PSYCHOANALYSIS AND SOCIETY

The Social Thought of Sigmund Freud

Arthur K. Berliner
Texas Christian University

UNIVERSITY
PRESS OF
AMERICA

Copyright © 1983 by
University Press of America, Inc.™
P.O. Box 19101, Washington, DC 20036

All rights reserved
Printed in the United States of America

ISBN (Perfect): 0-8191-2894-5
ISBN (Cloth): 0-8191-2893-7

UNIVERSITY
PRESS OF
AMERICA

To Miriam

Acknowledgements

In a moment of chastened reflection precipitated by the Bay of Pigs fiasco, President John Kennedy remarked, "There is an old saying that victory has a hundred fathers and defeat is an orphan." Insofar as completion of this book may represent a victory of sorts, there are indeed several people who rightly may claim a share of its ancestry.

Dr. Charles Glasgow of the North Texas State University Sociology Department first suggested to me that Sigmund Freud was a figure worthy of further sociological investigation, and encouraged me to pursue this inquiry as a doctoral dissertation. Dr. Leonard Benson, department chairman, directed the dissertation. He provided unfailing encouragement and support while offering incisive criticism of my work. His contribution was indispensable to completion of the study. Mary Alice Oatman typed the manuscript in its book form with diligence and accuracy. From inception of this study to its completion my wife, Miriam, performed a multifaceted role. During my moments of discouragement and self-doubt she conveyed to me her steadfast confidence in the outcome. She listened to my musings, read excerpts from the manuscript, and offered suggestions which helped me clarify what I was trying to say. I hope this study reflects to some degree the intelligence, good will, and affection of these kind and loyal people, who so sustained my efforts.

CONTENTS

	PAGE
ACKNOWLEDGEMENTS	v
PREFACE	ix

Chapter

I. INTRODUCTION: A BRIEF HISTORY OF SOCIOLOGICAL RESPONSES TO FREUDIAN THOUGHT ... 1

    A Historical Review

II. SOCIAL AND INTELLECTUAL ANTECEDENTS OF PSYCHOANALYTIC THOUGHT AND THE LIFE-CAREER OF SIGMUND FREUD ... 13

    European Intellectual History
    The European Medical Tradition:
      Romantic to Scientific Psychiatry
    The Unconscious
    Freud and His Times
    Freud's Personality and the
      Psychoanalytic Movement
    A Summing Up

III. FREUD'S CLINICAL THOUGHT AND SOCIAL WORKS ... 49

IV. SOCIETY: SOCIAL ORIGINS, SOCIAL CONTROL, AND SOCIAL CHANGE ... 63

    Social Origins and Social
      Change
    Social Reality and Social
      Cohesion
    Social Change

V. SOCIAL GROUPS, THE FAMILY AND
    RELIGION   105

        Social Groups
        Concluding Critique
        The Family
        A Critique of Freud's Views
          of the Family
        Religion
        Religion: Beyond Freud
          and Durkheim

VI. SIGMUND FREUD AS SOCIAL THEORIST   149

        Freud, Biological, Psychological
          and Social Man
        Freedom and Necessity in Freud's
          Thought
        Individual and Society: Freud
          and Parsons
        Sigmund Freud As Social Theorist

INDEX   193

ABOUT THE AUTHOR   205

PREFACE

At the time of his death in 1939 Sigmund Freud was one of the most famous figures in the western world. People in many walks of life, in many countries, had heard of him and talked about his ideas. However, as in the case of his great contemporary, Albert Einstein, many did not understand what his ideas were all about. Then, in ensuing decades, the growing influence of a systems perspective in psychology and social science tended to identify individualistic theories as anachronistic and to diminish Freud to the status of a historical curiosity.

Social science never has been at ease with this forbidding figure whose "libertine" ideas contrasted so starkly with his personal behavior. Freud's reputation has not been enhanced by his strictures on women and his derogation of the United States as a matriarchal culture. He has been seen in a narrower and narrower framework, as one whose distorted vision of man accorded no place to the "higher" human attributes. Freud was criticized for neglecting the social context within which human behavior was shaped and expressed. Psychiatry, Clinical Psychology and Social Work, where Freud's ideas previously had exercised a compelling, if not dominating influence, now seemed to find new sources of inspiration.

Nevertheless, Freud's influence on the healing/counseling disciplines and in other realms--anthropology, philosophy, art, literature--has persisted. Moreover some awareness existed that, in his later years, Freud had enlarged his interests beyond strictly clinical concerns, to write about "cultural and historical problems--ultimately the great problem of how man came to be what he is." In pursuit of this endeavor Freud wrote a series of books which addressed social themes. While clinicians tended to ignore them as extraneous to the main body of psychoanalytic thought, these works did attract some attention from social scientists. The most notable responses of which I am aware are Philip Rieff's <u>Freud: The Mind of the Moralist</u> (1959) and

Paul Roazen's <u>Freud</u>, <u>Political</u> <u>and</u> <u>Social Thought</u> (1968). I have made considerable use of both in this study.

Even the thoughts of geniuses do not germinate without fertile soil and benevolent climate. While transcending the time and cultural space of his origins Freud remained a product of those forces which influenced such other nineteenth century notables as Charles Darwin, whom he much admired, and Karl Marx, whom he apparently ignored. Since the currents of thought preceding Freud, and extant in his time, did much to shape his thinking, this study considers these influences as well as those of his family background. Because Freud's clinical thought constituted the point of departure of many of his social ideas, a brief resume of his concepts of individual mental structure and functioning is provided. The book then undertakes a content analysis of Freud's major social essays: <u>Totem and Taboo</u>, <u>Group Psychology and the Analysis of the Ego</u>, <u>The Future of an Illusion</u>, <u>Civilization and Its Discontents</u> and <u>Moses and Monotheism</u>. From these sources Freud's ideas about human societies and major social institutions were gleaned.

Social origins, social control, and social change, social groups, the family, and religion are examined from Freud's standpoint, and his ideas critiqued. Freud and Emile Durkheim and Freud and Karl Marx are compared on certain dimensions of their thought. Finally, an estimate is made of Freud's contributions and limitations as a social theorist.

To the end of his life Freud persisted in his quest to understand man and his culture. During his last sixteen years he faced, unflinchingly, an implacable enemy--a cancer of the jaw and palate which ultimately killed him. He suffered some thirty operations and a cumbersome prosthesis which, together with the disease itself, sometimes induced excruciating pain. Nevertheless, he refused any medication lest it cloud his mind and interfere with his work. His affliction seemed an irony worthy of Greek drama in that Freud, inventor of a "talking cure," developed an ailment which at times made it impossible for him to speak. This is reminiscent of the fate of another splendid innovator. Beethoven, a supremely gifted composer, lost his hearing. Both men remained dedicated to their creative work. One need not be a "Freudian" to admire an individual of such unshakeable resolve and high attainment.

CHAPTER I

INTRODUCTION: A BRIEF HISTORY OF SOCIOLOGICAL RESPONSES TO FREUDIAN THOUGHT

The purpose of this study is to analyze and synthesize the social thought of Sigmund Freud. Freud's reputation as the pioneering genius of depth psychology rests secure. However, other dimensions of his work, appearing in his later years, await systematic study. This work contained ideas of import to social science. Freud addressed such issues as socialization processes, social organization and social structure, and social control and social change. These aspects of his thought merit further exposition.

Freud belongs among those giants of the western intellectual tradition who introduced revolutionary views of man. Nicholas Copernicus (1473-1543) demonstrated that the earth, man's world, is not the center of the universe. Charles Darwin (1809-1882) documented the fact that man is not a special creation but an evolving member of the animal kingdom. And Freud (1856-1939) climaxed this progressive "dethronement" of man through systematic observations which identified and classified the irrational sources of man's behavior. Thereby he contributed to the sequence of innovative paradigms which in Thomas Kuhn's view[1] underlies the progress of scientific thought.

A Historical Review

Sociological interest in Freud and psychoanalysis goes back to the early decades of this century.[2]

However, this interest has emphasized the application of Freud's <u>clinical</u> discoveries to areas of sociological concern. Sociology has not yet focused upon the explication of Freud's social thought. The latter ideas are found in a body of work published mainly between 1912 and 1939, i.e., following the period of Freud's great clinical discoveries. The mature Freud, while continuing to work and write about psychopathology, now extended the reach of his thought to wider realms: human groupings, religion, society, and civilization itself. These works of Freud's later years largely have been ignored by social scientists who have tended to view them as essays in social criticism or metapsychology. Thus Freud's importance for the understanding of social phenomena has not gained the recognition accorded his studies of individual behavior. This essay attempts to remedy the hiatus.

Freud visited the United States by invitation in 1909 to lecture at Clark University. An impressive array of notables, including William James and G. Stanley Hall, attended the introduction of psychoanalysis to the American scene. Sociologists, like their colleagues in other behavioral sciences, were intrigued by Freud's ideas. Some of the leading sociologists attempted to link Freud's clinical discoveries with existing sociological thought. This early rapproachment has been described by Hinkle[3] who studied the period 1909-1935. A review of her work and of the more recent sociological literature reveals a progression in sociologists' use of Freudian ideas.

Freud's influence in American sociology reflects developments within the discipline itself. The interaction occurred in three phases. The early period, from 1909 to about 1920, was characterized by the use of psychoanalytic concepts to buttress the prevailing individualistic orientation of sociology. During the subsequent, middle period, covering the early twenties to the late forties a more varied response evolved. Clinical psychoanalysis continued to exert some influence. However, an emerging trend in sociology, toward empiricism, tended over time to discredit psychoanalysis, for the latter's constructs eluded rigorous testing. On the other hand, the biographical emphasis in the psychoanalytic technique encouraged initiation of the life-history method in sociological studies.[4] The recent phase, occurring during the nineteen fifties to the nineteen seventies, reflected a more mature sociological perspective. Sociologists, rather than merely borrowing, now attempted to integrate psychoanalytic concepts with those of sociology. And a number of books by sociologists surveying the development and range of sociological thought included chapters or sections dealing with Freud's theories. However, during this decades-long period of sociological interest in psychoanalysis no systematic study of Freud's social thought, per se, had been undertaken.

Any recognition of Freud as a social theorist remained dormant during the early relationship between psychoanalysis and sociology. Freud's clinical discoveries were applied to the individualistic interpretation of social behavior then prevalent in American sociology. Freud's stress on the psychic determinism of social behavior meshed well with the basic tenets of the founders of the American Sociological Society. Both saw social behavior as derivative of the mental mechanisms of individuals; sublimation of individual drives induced behaviors which led to social change.[5] Also, individual and society were seen in conflict, engaged in a "collision between [individual] instincts and . . . group control."[6]

Developments of the middle period (early twenties to late forties) evoked significant changes in the relationship between psychoanalysis and sociology. The developments, while widening somewhat the scope of application of Freudian theories, retained the original orientation, i.e., Freud's contribution to sociology still was seen in terms of his clinical work. Freud's insistence that human behavior rests basically upon emotional foundations and is produced by psychic causes had been "verified" by the collective irrationality of the first World War. Conviction about this irrationality was strengthened among social scientists. Disillusioned concerning the idea of progress, they sought the hidden wellsprings of human behavior. W. F. Ogburn in 1923 published an article interpreting in psychoanalytic terms the prevalence of irrationalism and its significance for the social sciences.[7]

Freud's theories of unconscious motivation and of repression exerted considerable influence. Thomas and Znaniecki stated

Society is, indeed, an agent for the repression of many of the wishes in the individual; it demands that he shall be moral by repressing at least the wishes which are irreconcilable with the welfare of the group, but nevertheless, it provides the only medium within which any of his schemes or wishes can be gratified.[8]

The apposition of Freud's and Thomas' thought was recognized by other writers, including Park and Burgess[9] and Burgess.[10] So was the recognition that

the basic structure of the Freudian theory of personality . . . was homologous to Cooley's theory of personal evolution through primary groups. . . .[11]

During the same period, however, the trend in sociology toward empiricism began to undermine the significance of Freudian thought for sociology. "Instinct" and other biologically based theories, upon which Freud's work was presumed to rest, either were considered disproved or defied empirical testing. Ethnological data developed during the twenties contributed to this depreciation of psychoanalysis. Ellsworth Faris,[12,13] Bronislaw Malinowski,[14] Margaret Mead[15] and others identified family constellations, sexual attitudes and interpersonal relationships in preliterate societies which cast doubt upon, or appeared to refute, the universality of the fixed, innate drives in man Freud had postulated.

Hinkle's study of the relationship between psychoanalysis and sociology spanned the years 1909-1935. With the exception of Moses and Monotheism all of Freud's social essays had already appeared. Nevertheless, her substantial bibliography contains Freud's clinical writings only. The obvious inference--that Freud's contribution to sociology during this period was viewed as related to his clinical work only--supports what has thus far been suggested, that regard for Freud continued to rest upon his psychology without consideration of his potential contribution to social thought. To the next generation of sociologists fell the task of undertaking a more sophisticated appraisal of Freud's significance for social thought.

Louis Schneider[16] in The Freudian Psychology and Veblen's Social Theory and Talcott Parsons came closer than had their predecessors to appreciating the larger scope of Freud's thought. Said Parsons:

> Had Freud lived long enough to enter more deeply into the technical analysis of the object-systems to which the individual becomes related, he would inevitably have had to become, in part, a sociologist, for the structure of these object-systems is--not merely is influenced by--the structure of the society itself. Essentially, Freud's theory of object-relations is a theory of the relation of the individual personality to the social system. It is a primary meeting ground of the two disciplines of psychology and sociology.[17]

Even here, Freud's contribution was still conceived in terms of a blending of two related disciplines--"a theory of the relation of the individual personality to the social system," in Parsons' words, rather than as a system of social thought in its own right.

Alvin Gouldner suggested that Parsons' effort to deal with the issue of social change by adducing the concept of a "resistance to change" has a "specific origin . . . in Freudian theory."[18] This passing reference to Freud and social change presaged appreciation of Freud as a social theorist. In his critique of Functionalism, Gouldner commented that, for the individual, this perspective neglects the costs of conformity and fails to see the rewards of deviance. Freudian thought, on the other hand, is directed toward freeing "men from out-moded social and character structures and, through this, to . . . greater fulfillment and development."[19]

Don Martindale has credited "Freudianism" as a source of certain types of "sociological formulations," i.e., "as a form of sociological theory which fused voluntaristic organicism and positivism very similar to Pareto's theory."[20] Martindale identifies a number of Freud's works which have particular relevance for sociology, and asserts that, although Freud's data sources for theory building were suspect, he did conceive of a basic social institution, the family, as "absolutely essential to the development of personality."[21] Martindale further establishes linkages between Freudian and sociological thought in the thinking of Gerth and Mills, and specifically their work on Character and Social Structure. "Gerth and Mills trace their affinities primarily to Mead and Freud."[22]

> Mead's concept of the generalized other and Freud's superego--their closest point of contact--enable us to link the private and the public, the innermost acts of the individual with the widest kinds of social-historical phenomena.'[23]

Finally, Martindale points to another example of the fruitfulness for social thought of Freud's ideas. This concerns Merton's construct of manifest and latent functions. Martindale asserts that Merton's employment of these terms, conceived sociologically,[24] is close to the meaning originally introduced by Freud.[25] The latter first described manifest (intended) and latent (unrecognized) dream content in The Interpretation of Dreams, published in 1900.

R. P. Cuzzort and E. W. King point out that Freud's thought has raised (without answering very satisfactorily) a fundamental question for social scientists. How does it happen that

> we develop communities that do not represent our 'natural' character and are, in many ways, antithetical to that character[?] How could any community develop to the point where it possesses a force greater than the biological reality of human nature?[26]

And in support of an observation previously made, Cuzzort and King suggest that the Freudian superego, as a product of community standards, transforms the biological organism into a social being; thus the superego imparts "sociological significance"[27] to Freudian thought.

Randall Collins and Michael Makowsky believe that Freud's significance for social thought is reflected in a number of ways. Two may be cited.

> Since Freud's pioneering psychiatric
> work, forms of mental illness . . .
> have come to be viewed largely as
> socially conditioned.[28]

and

> It is only through the process of
> socialization, when the child begins to
> internalize the parents' values . . .
> that the child learns to . . . tailor
> himself to social norms.[29]

As Freud's work progressed he became convinced that mental phenomena could not be reduced to a somatic base; they existed as psychological entities in themselves. His later thought also indicated awareness of the influence of culture. For example, he acknowledged that the period of latency, i.e., the "interruption" of childhood sexual life, occurs only in social organizations which suppress infantile sexuality. Even resolution of the Oedipus complex, in Freud's own view the centerpiece of his theory of personality development, required a critical interpersonal transaction for its resolution, viz., the child's substitution of identification for hostility in its attitude toward the parent of the same sex. Thus Freud himself recognized clearly that personality dynamics could be modified by social relationships.

Freud was a seminal thinker. Diverse realms of contemporary western culture--art, literature, political science, history, philosophy, etc.--have been suffused with his ideas. Nor did he leave sociology unaffected, as has been indicated above. Nevertheless, his contributions to the understanding of human groups and human social organization still await systematic exposition. Such an effort may contribute toward the development of a social science paradigm or model of society better attuned to Freudian constructs.

This study will analyze the content of a selected group of Freud's essays which dealt with themes relevant to social science. The major essays are identified in the next section. The analysis will focus upon identifying the Freudian view of the origins and functioning of society and of certain social institutions, the family and religion; also data will be sought on the phenomena of social control and social change.

Several problems are apparent. Freud was not a social scientist, and he did not express his social thought in social science language. Moreover, though he possessed superb language skills both in German[30] and English he often used the metaphors of nineteenth century physics to characterize mental functioning and human behavior. Thus another layer of complexity must be penetrated to understand his relevance for contemporary social thought. Also, Freud's translators, it may be argued, seem not to have used the most felicitous expressions in rendering some of Freud's key concepts. This raises questions concerning Freud's basic orientation. Was he, in fact, as biologically oriented as the consistent translation of <u>Trieb</u> into "Instinct" would suggest?

These are not insurmountable obstacles. However, they reinforce the conviction that content analysis must seek the large picture which Freud portrayed, his <u>Weltanschauung</u>, rather than the minutiae of his thoughts. In so doing we may discover that Freud's "science" of human behavior will bear as much resemblance to philosophy as to social science. The objective of this study, therefore, is to analyze Freud's social thought, to synthesize the threads of his several essays into a coherent fabric of thought. This will help provide an answer to where Freud belongs vis-a-vis social science.

Freud wrote voluminously and in many areas. His published books and essays represent only part of his output. Several large volumes of correspondence exist, as do other items: addresses to various groups, oral presentations, etc. This study will be confined to the analysis of his five avowedly social works, published in the order listed below, as well as several articles which also deal with social themes. The books are

<u>Totem and Taboo</u> (1912-13)
<u>Group Psychology and the Analysis of the Ego</u>(1921)
<u>The Future of an Illusion</u> (1927)
<u>Civilization and its Discontents</u> (1929-30)
<u>Moses and Monotheism</u> (1939)

The Study has been organized as follows:

Chapter II: Social and Intellectual Antecedents
              of Psychoanalytic Thought and the
              Life-Career of Sigmund Freud

Chapter III: Freud's Clinical Thought and Social
              Works

Chapter IV: Society: Social Origins, Social
              Control, and Social Change

Chapter V: Social Groups, The Family, and
              Religion

Chapter VI: Sigmund Freud as Social Theorist

   In the following chapter we examine the influences, both ideological and familial, which helped shape Freud's intellectual interests and the direction of his thought.

NOTES

[1] Thomas Kuhn, The Structure of Scientific Revolution, 22nd Ed. (Chicago: University of Chicago Press, 1970).

[2] Thomas D. Eliot, "A Psychoanlytic Interpretation of Group Formation and Behavior," American Journal of Sociology 26, November 1920, 333-352.

[3] Gisela J. Hinkle, "The Role of Freudianism in American Sociology." unpublished Ph.D. Dissertation (University of Wisconsin, 1951).

[4] Clifford Shaw, The Jack Roller (Chicago: University of Chicago Press, 1930).

[5] Hinkle, op. cit., pp. 38, 39.

[7] W. F. Ogburn, "Bias, Psychoanalysis and the Subjective in Relation to the Social Sciences," Publications of the American Sociological Society, XVII, 1923, pp. 62-74.

[8] W. I. Thomas and F. Znaniecki, The Polish Peasant in Europe and America, Vol. I, quoted in Hinkle, op. cit., 85.

[9] R. E. Park and E. W. Burgess, Introduction to the Science of Sociology, VII, 1924, p. 96.

[10] E. W. Burgess, "Family Study," in L. L. Bernard (ed.) The Fields and Methods of Sociology (New York: Farar & Rinehart, Inc., 1934), p. 454.

[11] Hinkle, op. cit., p. 251.

[12] E. Faris, "Are Instincts Data or Hypotheses?", American Journal of Sociology, XXVII, September 1921.

[13] E. Faris, "Ethnological Light on Psychological Problems," Publications of the American Sociological Society, XVI, 1922, pp. 113-120.

[14] Bronislaw Malinowski, Sex and Repression in Primitive Society, (New York: Harcourt, Brace & Co., 1927).

[15] Margaret Mead, Coming of Age in Samoa (New York: William Morrow & Co., 1928).

[16] Louis Schneider, The Freudian Psychology and Veblen's Social Theory (New York: King's Crown Press, 1948), p. 54.

[17] Talcott Parsons, "Social Structure and the Development of Personality: Freud's Contribution to the Integration of Psychology and Sociology," Psychiatry, No. 4, November 1958, p. 321.

[18] Alvin W. Gouldner, The Coming Crisis in Western Sociology (New York: Basic Books, Inc., 1970), p. 38.

[19] Ibid., p. 355.

[20] Don Martindale, The Nature and Types of Sociological Theory (Boston: Houghton Mifflin Co., 1960), p. 105.

[21] Ibid., p. 106.

[22] Ibid., p. 370.

[23] Hans Gerth and C. Wright Mills, Character and Social Structure, op. cit., p. 370.

[24] Robert F. Merton, Social Theory and Social Structure (Glencoe, Illinois: The Free Press, 1949), P. 51.

[25] Martindale, op. cit., p. 474.

[26] R. P. Cuzzort and E. W. King, Humanity and Modern Social Thought, 2nd Ed. (Hinsdale, Illinois: Dryden Press, 1976), p.90.

[27] Ibid.

[28] Randall Collins and Michael Makowsky, The Discovery of Society, 2nd ed., rev. (New York: Random House, 1978), p. 140.

[29] Ibid., p. 142.

[30] Thomas Mann described Freud as one of the great stylists of European literature.

CHAPTER II

SOCIAL AND INTELLECTUAL ANTECEDENTS OF PSYCHOANALYTIC THOUGHT AND THE LIFE-CAREER OF SIGMUND FREUD

This chapter traces the major social and intellectual tributaries from which flowed the stream of Freudian thought. In addition, those aspects of Freud's life and career influential in shaping his psychoanalytic and social thought will be delineated.

Innovative conceptions often trace an extensive lineage. Freud's discoveries are no exception. For example, Denis Diderot, in a work published in 1772, eighty-four years before Freud's birth, commented that the undeniable benefits of civilization had been secured at the price of mankind's happiness. Civilized man, according to his argument, is a product of internal conflict between "natural man" and "moral and artificial man."[1] Regardless of the outcome, man is doomed to inevitable unhappiness. This idea subsequently emerged in the thought of Friedrich Nietzsche (1844-1900)--and, later, in that of Sigmund Freud.

Psychoanalytic thought originated as a late nineteenth century phenomenon, the antecedents of which may be traced through three major referrents: developments in European intellectual history beginning in the 18th century; the 19th century European medical tradition; and the evolution of the idea of the "Unconscious." Each of these sources will be examined.

European Intellectual History

A number of developments in European intellectual history during the century and a half preceding Freud are linked to the development of his thought. These include the movements known as the Enlightenment, Romanticism, Positivism, Darwinism and Marxism, and

13

Nietzschean philosophy. Each will be discussed and its influence on the development of Freud's thought will be indicated.

Europe in the early eighteenth century hovered on the brink of tremendous change. The great discoveries in the natural sciences culminating in the work of Newton supported belief in an orderly universe accessible to systematic investigation and rational thought. A new economic class, the bourgeoisie, was rising and consolidating its power. An outgrowth was the Enlightenment, a movement which assumed different emphases in different countries. Originating in France around 1730, the stress there lay in political and antireligious ideology; in England the focus lay in rationalizing the system of production; in Germany it produced a relaxation of political despotism. In common, however, was the Enlightenment's exaltation of reason and the belief that mankind now possessed the key to unlimited progress through the application of a secularized science to the reform of society. Society existed for man, and progress, both material and moral, required use of science and education, rather than reliance upon authority and tradition. If the natural world was amenable to understanding through the scientific method, so should the human mind, society and political organization. Rousseau (1712-1778), a representative of Enlightenment thought, essayed a reconstruction of the evolution of society, which he hypothesized developed when individuals came together to conclude a "social contract."

The Enlightenment furthered the development of international scientific communion, religious tolerance, and reform on a number of fronts--judicial and penal reform, for example. Most notably, for purposes of this study, medical reforms were inaugurated which precipitated psychiatry out of its era of devil possession into its first attempts to see mental illness as a disturbance of reason. Its causes were sought principally in some lesion of the brain.

With its espousal of freedom of religion and thought and human equality, and a conception of the state as a political organization which served the rights and needs of the ordinary citizen, the Enlightenment represented a watershed in western civilization. Modern psychiatry sprang from its impulse. However, there also were less positive effects. The Enlightenment tended to overlook individual human differences and ignored cultural diversity. Enlightenment science combined rationalism with irrational speculation. A prevalent preoccupation involved the search for the primitive world which presumably existed at the origin of mankind, a world presumed to be of unparalleled knowledge and wisdom.[2] By about 1785 the vision of the Enlightenment had begun to wane. Nevertheless, its influence was never eclipsed. The extolling of human reason and the scientific method became premanently embedded in the western tradition, and Sigmund Freud, in his time, absorbed this aspect of the Enlightenment.

A cultural reaction against the Enlightenment originated in Germany early in the nineteenth century. France, England, and other countries soon experienced its influence. In opposition to the Enlightenment's elevation of reason as a supreme value, and its concern with society, Romanticism espoused the cult of the irrational and of the individual. In its political expression Romanticism supported nationalism and national identiy. In contrast with the Enlightenment's belief that "The proper study of mankind is man," Romanticism, responding to the political, economic, and demographic disequilibrium in Germany, turned to nature as a central focus. Man's relationship to nature replaced man's relationship to society as a central concern. And nature's secrets could be penetrated through non-rational processes of mind, and through attention to dreams, myths, and other spontaneous expressions of human volition.

In contrast with the Enlightenment, Romanticism placed strong emphasis on the idea of the Individual and his absolute uniqueness. The Weltanschauung of each contrasts diametrically: In the Enlightenment view society was the voluntary, artificial product of reasoned human wills joined in a social contract; Romanticism held that man's communal existence was a "given" of nature, independent of man's will. Moreover, nature could not be understood by means of mechanical and physical concepts; the underlying spiritual laws must be apprehended. Nature constituted a harmonious whole and man existed in cosmic harmony with nature. An essential principle of this philosophy of nature was the "law of polarities." In nature one found day and night, force and matter, male and female.[3] Ernest Jones, Freud's disciple, friend and biographer, observed that Freud's concepts of mental life were dominated by polarities. Thus, he wrote of <u>Eros</u> and <u>Thanatos</u> (life and death) instincts, subject and object, pleasure and unpleasure, active and passive. Characteristic in Freud's thinking throughout his life was "his constant proclivity to dualistic ideas,"[4] strongly reminiscent of Romantic thinking.

Like the Enlightenment which preceded it, Romanticism was destined to run its course, although as was the case with its forerunner, it left its impress on later generations. The revolutionary upheavals of the nineteenth century, both political and socioeconomic, led, by 1850, to a new ideological synthesis. The Industrial Revolution was now in full flow. A vast increase in the production of goods and new means of transportation accelerated the trend toward urbanization. The two processes--urbanization and industrialization--produced a new social class, the proletariat. The bourgeoisie, increasingly conscious of the perceived threat from below, were confronted in 1848 by the Communist Manifesto and a growing socialist movement.

The world increasingly assumed a configuration of sovereign national entities. The nationalistic ferment stimulated by Romanticism was beginning to threaten the great multinational empires. And a new philosophy was emerging, that of <u>Positivism</u>. Its origins lay with the French Encyclopedists of the eighteenth century, particularly Condorcet, "who contended that the progress of the human mind would be achieved through the progress of science."[5]

The new world view was inaugurated by St. Simon early in the nineteenth century and systematized by August Comte in France and by John Stuart Mill (whose works Freud later translated into German), and Herbert Spencer in England. Rejecting Romanticism's speculative bent, Postivism believed in the supreme virtue of facts; constant laws, naively believed to have been discovered in physics, were to be derived for human societies through experimental methods. Following the precedent laid down in Enlightenment thought, Positivism's concern was with man as a social creature.

Thanks to the influence of Positivism, the burgeoning scientific research in universities, and the generally prevailing optimistic outlook, an unprecendented faith in science developed. Progress in inventions and discoveries during the latter half of the nineteenth century encouraged an almost religious faith in the powers of science and a growing trend toward atheism. Freud's denigration of religion, his faith in science, and in the ultimate discovery of laws of development of man and society reflected this positivist influence.

The great social and political changes in the western world during the nineteenth century, especially after 1850, required new ideologies. Romanticism was waning. The Enlightenment was in decline. The related phenomena of the Industrial Revolution, free enterprise, competition, the struggle for world markets, found a seemingly scientific rationalization in the work of Charles Darwin (1809-1882), who had hypothesized a pattern of differential survival and procreation rates among animal species based upon their capacities to adapt to changing environmental conditions. Karl Marx (1818-1883) meanwhile was engaged in constructing an ideological foundation for the socialist parties developing in response to a growing industrial proletariat and rising class consciousness. Darwinism and Marxism exerted tremendous influence in the European world after 1860. This was the world in which Sigmund Freud grew to maturity. Freud never alluded to Marx in the works analyzed in this study and he dismissed the Soviet state as naive in its conception of human nature. Freud's own thought clearly indicated he was influenced by some of the same intellectual currents as was Marx. A comparison of the two theorists appears in the last chapter of this study.

For Enlightenment thinkers progress was a continuous process in which human reason would achieve mankind's resulting happiness. Romantic thinkers, too, saw a rational aim at work, propelled though it was by unconscious, irrational forces of nature. Now Darwinism called attention to the social and moral progress of mankind as a consequence of biological progress among species, based upon a blind, universal struggle. However,

The most important influence of Darwinism was felt through <u>Social Darwinism</u>, that is, the indiscriminate application of the concepts of 'struggle for life,' 'survival of the fittest,' and 'elimination of the unfit' to the facts and problems of human societies.

This line of thought, which could be traced from Hobbes' principle of 'man is a wolf to man' to Malthus [and then to Darwin] . . . gave its specific coloring to the Western world particularly in the last decades of the nineteenth and the beginning of the twentieth centuries.6

Freud, like many of his well educated contemporaries, read Darwin and reacted with enthusiasm. Darwin's thought had significant impact on Freud in two respects. Darwin's conjecture about a primal horde as the characteristic state of primitive man provided Freud a starting point for the development of his own theory of social origins; the English naturalist's hypothesis about the universality of intrapecies conflict became embedded in Freud's theories about man being in a perpetual state of conflict with and within his society.

The world of the late nineteenth century, circa 1880, placed strong emphasis on male domination. Political rights and the world of work outside the home were essentially not available to women. Not until the early 1890's was a university education available to women. "Male" virtues of ambition, aggressiveness, and virility were emphasized in literary works. Patriarchal authority was unchallenged; educational procedures were authoritarian, reflecting the family norm of the despotic father. Generational conflict, especially between fathers and sons, was frequent. Authoritarianism

> was a feature of the times and reigned everywhere . . . . Laws were more repressive, delinquent youth sternly punished and corporal punishment was considered indispensable. All this must be considered with regard to the genesis of Freud's Oedipus complex.7

18

Freud shared this sex-typed view of male superiority and it was reflected in his writings on the origins and significance of religion, family structure, and the dynamics of group life.

Thus, a century ago, around 1880, during the young manhood of Sigmund Freud, the most progressive elements in the western world seemed firmly in the grip of positivism and evolutionism and cherished its belief in the all-conquering power of science. Then, around 1885, "a marked change in intellectual orientation could be felt throughout Europe."[8] The change was reflected in the work of Friedrich Nietzsche (1844-1900). In such works as <u>Genealogy of Morals</u>[9] Nietzsche considered the human mind as a system of drives, and emotions were regarded as having unconscious derivations. Nietzsche could be characterized as a conspicuous representative of a trend prevalent in the 1880's, the "uncovering" or "unmasking" psychology also now reflected in contemporary literature, e.g., in the work of Dostoevsky and Ibsen. Man, said Nietzsche, is a self-deceiving and other-deceiving creature.

Nietzsche explained civilization's origin as synonymous with the origin of conscience, based upon renunciation of instinctual gratifications. Civilization is

> The consequence of a forcible separation from the animal past, . . . a declaration of war against the old instincts, which, up to then constituted [man's] strength, his pleasure, and his awesomeness.[10]

The generation of Freud's childhood had been imbued with Darwinian thought. The generation of his young maturity was permeated with the thought of Nietzsche. Freud, himself, referred to this philosopher as one "whose guesses and intuitions often agree in the most astonishing way with the laborious findings of psychoanalysis;" Freud went on to say that for a considerable time he eschewed studying Nietzsche to avoid being influenced by him.[11] The fact Freud avoided reading Nietzsche probably made no difference for his ideas saturated the intellectual thought of the time and were widely reported in the media.

Psychoanalysis became a part of the "unmasking" trend of the 1880's and 1890's in which words and deeds manifested not their literal selves but represented, for both Nietzsche and Freud, unconscious motivations and conflicts. The unconscious was inhabited by those drives denied normative expression, drives derived from the early life of mankind and of the individual, and which assert themselves in dreams, mental illness, and other psychic manifestations. Nietzsche not only arrived at notions of mind as a system of drives possessing energy which could be inhibited, released, or displaced from one object to another; additionally, he had given expression to the ideas of Id (das Es) and the term Ego.[12]

Nietzsche's undoubted influence did not, however, dissipate the powerful hold of "scientism," the belief that in science lay the only valid answers to the great problems of the time. The dominant sciences were the natural ones. These strongly reinforced beliefs in materialism and atheism. Religion was considered an ally of such reactionary forces as tradition, superstition, and anti-science.

> Historically, the period from 1850-1900 was noteworthy as an era when an old power, religion, and a relatively new rival, science [divided up] the universe . . . . The duality of interest and approach which implicitly said that science must avoid contact with the so-called spiritual values while reserving for itself its concern with material reality was the strongest force in the intellectual world . . . .[13]

What did science have to say about the human mind? Mind was conceived as a

> function of organic structure, of inherited disposition and tensions . . . . This view [was a product of] the mechanistic-evolutionary intellectual climate of the late nineteenth century reinforced by a preoccupation with such purely biological concepts as instinct, race, maturation, etc. . . . . Environmental forces are primarily stimuli which evoke, or only modify

> . . . developmental trends . . . that unfold from within the organism itself. They are not basic constituents of mind or behavior.[14]

The European Medical Tradition: Romantic to Scientific Psychiatry

Although Freud, in later years, claimed that doctors were poor candidates for the role of psychoanalyst,[15] it was medicine which provided the immediate context for development of psychoanalytic thought. Nineteenth century medicine, thanks to progress in the basic sciences, focused upon defining diseases and determining their physical causes. Pasteur's work in bacteriology had pointed the way by correlating disease agents with specific diagnostic entities. Emotions, thoughts and behavior were presumed to reflect underlying organic processes.

> By the last third of the nineteenth century, psychiatry . . . looked for . . . organic pathology. This development was promoted by the discovery of pathological lesions in the brains of psychotic individuals . . . .
>
> It was from this general medical and psychiatric background that Freud came to the study of the Neuroses.[16]

The latter part of the nineteenth century, however, represented a reaction against the "Romantic Psychiatry" which had dominated European psychiatric thought during the late eighteenth and first half of the nineteenth century. Romantic psychiatry, so called because it occurred concurrently, and was influenced by, the European Romantic era, flourished in close connection with philosophy. The dominant theme of the latter, intrigued as it was by a belief in the basic unity of all life, saw nature as comprehensible in somewhat mystical terms. This view held that

> The whole of the universe and of being, human and all other, is bound together in an all-pervading, all-meaningful relatedness, and only in this relatedness is any portion of the total to be comprehended.[17]

Romantic psychiatry, spanning the period about 1780-1840, engrossed with

> irrational, emotional, and hidden forces of the human personality . . . keenly interested in [patients'] actual thoughts and feelings . . . believed that mental disease was a result of the individual's psychological development. [It] held beliefs now considered quite sophisticated: the notion of inner conflict; . . . the human being as a psychobiological entity; that idea can become symbolized and expressed in physical reactions . . . .[18]

Romantic psychiatry, preoccupied with philosophical questions, came to rely on <u>a priori</u> reasoning and a variety of mystical beliefs. Some adherents believed that mental illness represented God's punishment for sin. Some espoused vitalism. A psychiatric literature developed "at once speculative, moralistic, and theological."[19] One important consequence was that philosophers came to preempt the fields of psychopathology and psychotherapy. Decker cites an interesting example. When an eminent physician of the day wrote a text on public health

> he sent a copy to Immanuel Kant (1724-1804)--soliciting . . . opinions of the book's sections on mental hygiene . . . because Kant had proposed his own classification of mental diseases . . . Kant believed that a philosopher was more of an authority on mental disturbances than was a physician. Kant insisted that expert psychiatric witnesses in criminal cases . . . should be invited from the faculty of philosophy and not from the medical faculty.[20]

Decker adds that Kant seldom was challenged in this assertion.

In the reaction against the Romantics' absorption with metaphysics, psychiatrists of the late nineteenth century embraced a more empirical position but in the process abandoned the insights of their Romantic predecessors. After 1850 energies were directed toward collecting and classifying data, and fitting these into a paradigm of mental illness as an affliction of the nervous system.[21] Most psychiatrists of the late nineteenth century were indifferent to issues of psychic conflict, the role of emotions in mental illness, the meaning of symbols, and unconscious processes. This attitude had to be of momentous importance for the later reaction to psychoanalysis.

Romantic psychiatry had

> focused on the individual and on his unique response--on the basis of his personality--to an individual approach. [Now] organically oriented psychiatry focused on the common <u>Anlage</u> [hereditary predisposition] of each individual and on the common means geared to modify a pathological condition uniformly affecting each individual.[22]

Organic or "scientific" psychiatry succeeded in dominating psychiatric thought in the latter half of the nineteenth century largely through the influence of several, principally German, scientists who led the reaction against teleological explanations of behavior. "No other forces than the common physical-chemical ones are active within the organism,"[23] became their rallying cry. Experimentation and observation would suffice to unravel the mysteries of life. Darwin's theory of natural selection, appearing in 1859, helped to lay the ghost of vitalism and telelogy. Effects could be derived only from physical causes. This was explanation enough.

> The experimental laboratory [now] entered the field of medicine. It soon became the . . . integral part of medicine . . . . Everywhere this great change was felt . . . . The great ambition [of nineteenth century psychiatrists], . . . to make [psychiatry] a legitimate branch of general medicine or neurology seemed . . . to have entered the phase of actual fulfillment.[24]

With confident assurance it could now be asserted that "mental disease is brain disease; various emotional aberrations are but signs of one disease, brain disease."25 In the flush of these new certainties the unconscious, wish fulfillment, the emotions seemed to have been relegated permanently to the realm of epiphenomena. But, even as Freud later was to characterize the ego as a soft, yet persistent voice, so the unconscious continued to press for recognition as a force to be reckoned with in human affairs. To this subject we now turn briefly.

The Unconscious

Freud's name and the unconscious appear indissolubly linked. Nevertheless, interest in and awareness of the unconscious far antedates him. However, only a cursory survey of pre-Freudian thought on this subject will be undertaken. Ellenberger26 and Decker27 have provided numerous citations of literary and philosophical figures who, prior to Freud, expressed ideas concerning the unconscious, as well as referring to contemporary psychiatrists and social scientists who have collated earlier writings about the unconscious. Mention may be made of

> the physician and philosopher, Ernst Platner (1744-1818), who not only asserted that unconscious ideas exist, but that they could be responsible for conscious ideas . . . . And even [earlier] . . . . In 1725 Wolff wrote that he objected to the Cartesian belief that nothing could be in the mind of which it is not aware.28

Even the idea had appeared that conscious and unconscious components of mind not only exist but do so in a state of conflict. Schopenhauer (1788-1860), as early as 1819, had described man as an irrational being dominated by internal forces whose existence man failed to understand. A contemporary, Carl Gustav Carus (1789-1869) published in 1846 a work, entitled Psyche, which attempted a comprehensive theory of unconscious psychological life. In it he stated that "the key to the knowledge of the nature of the soul's conscious life lies in the realm of the unconscious. . . . ."29 Growing awareness of the unconscious was furthered by the publication of Eduard Von Hartmann's The Philosophy of the Unconscious in 1859. As Collins and Makowsky point out, Hartmann's philosophy of "will" and "intellect" engaged in conflict paralleled Freud's later formulations of "id" versus "ego."[30]

Whyte, a historian of social thought, avers that by "1870-1880 the general concept of the unconscious mind was a European commonplace."[31] By the time Freud in 1900 in The Interpretation of Dreams had presented his own ideas concerning the unconscious his work represented the culmination of an extensive literary and philosophical tradition. Insofar as Freud's ideas about the unconscious generated controversy and resistance the source lay not in the assertion of an unconscious; as has been pointed out the idea of the unconscious was hardly innovative. Rather, opposition stemmed from the alleged unscientific character of the concept and its presumed reduction of man's creativity to the level of instinct. Meanwhile, it became Freud's task to advance not merely a hypothesis of the existence of unconscious mental processes but to document and support this assertion in the most innovative and compelling way. He replaced literary allusion and philosophical speculation with causal chain and empirical reasoning. As will be seen in the account of Freud's life which follows, there were a number of sources for the controversy over and resistance toward psychoanalysis and Freud's version of the unconscious.

Freud and His Times

Sigmund Freud was born May 6, 1856, in Freiberg, Moravia, then a part of the Austro-Hungarian empire, now in Czechoslovakia. He died in London in September, 1939. He lived an unusually long life span divided almost equally between two vastly dissimilar centuries. Most of our knowledge of Freud's life and social circumstances, as well as the prevailing intellectual currents through which his thought was filtered, are derived from secondary sources. Freud quite deliberately sought to confound any future biographers asserting he did not wish to make it easy for them. His An Autobiographical Study[32] written in 1924-25 essentially describes the development of his scientific career and thought and is sparing of personal data.

Freud was the first born child of the marriage of a forty-year-old widower and a twenty-year-old young woman. Freud had two step-brothers and seven younger siblings. When he was three the family was forced to move to Liepzig. His father, Jacob, a textile merchant, was ruined by one of the economic crises endemic in the transition from small manufacturing to large scale industry; there was the additional problem of anti-Semitism which flared up during these hard times. A year later, when Freud was four, the family moved to Vienna. Here Freud lived until the last year of his life when the Nazi terror again forced relocation, to Freud's beloved England, where the last year of his life was spent.

Jacob Freud never again regained the affluence of Freiberg and his large family was forced to live in a crowded apartment. Nevertheless, Sigmund, the oldest child, enjoyed a privileged position. Adored by his mother, who referred to him as "mein goldener Sigie" and, because of his scholarship, a source of pride to his more reserved father, Sigmund had his own room and an oil lamp (the others made do with candles).33 Once the ten-year old Sigmund complained of the noise of his sister's piano practice, the instrument was sold and that was the last of any music lessons in the family. Freud attributed his manifest self-confidence to his favored status.

> A man who has been the indisputable favorite of his mother keeps for life the feeling of a conqueror, that confidence of success that often induces real success.34

Freud received the whole of his education in Vienna. At the Gymnasium (roughly equivalent to American secondary schooling) he remained at the top of his class for all seven years and seldom was required to take examinations. Meanwhile visions of greatness danced in his head. He admired Hannibal, the "semitic" general, often enacted famous battles for his sisters and thought of a military career; alternatively, he thought of the legal profession with the goal of becoming a cabinet minister; a scientific career, too, attracted his interest. Ultimately his youthful enthusiasm settled on medicine.

> I was moved . . . by a sort of curiosity, which was directed more toward human concerns than toward natural objects; nor had I grasped the importance of observation as one of the best means of gratifying it. . . . At

> the same time, the theories of Darwin
> . . . strongly attracted me, for they
> held out hopes of an extraordinary
> advance in our understanding of the
> world; and it was hearing Goethe's
> beautiful essay on nature . . . just
> before I left school that decided me to
> become a medical student.[35]

At the University of Vienna Medical School, which Freud entered in 1873, he encountered his first direct and painful experience with anti-semitism.

> I found that I was expected to feel
> myself inferior and an alien because I
> was a Jew. I refused absolutely to do
> the first of these things. I have never
> been able to see why I should feel
> ashamed of my descent. . . . I put up,
> without much regret, with my
> non-acceptance into the community.
> . . . These first impressions at the
> University, however, had one consequence
> which was afterwards to prove important;
> for at an early age I was made familiar
> with the fate of being put under the ban
> of the 'compact majority.' The
> foundations were thus laid for a
> certain degree of independence of
> judgment.[36]

Freud's status as a marginal man may later have made it easier for him to break new intellectual ground.

This forthright affirmation of selfhood, noted above, contrasts strikingly with Freud's recollection of a story told the twelve-year old boy by his father. The latter, out walking, had his cap knocked off his head by a Gentile, with the imprecation, "Jew, get off the pavement!" "What did you do?" asked the indignant young Sigmund. "I went into the roadway and picked up my cap."[37] Freud felt his father had behaved disappointingly.

> I contrasted this situation with another
> which fitted my feelings better: the
> scene in which Hannibal's father . . .
> made his boy swear . . . to take
> vengeance on the Romans. Ever since
> . . . Hannibal had a place in my
> phantasies.[38]

This was but one indication of Freud's ambivalence toward his father. Erich Fromm believes this attitude is related significantly to the psychological system Freud created, e.g., the concept of the Oedipus complex, as well as to the later works which are the object of this study. In <u>Totem and Taboo</u> the primordial father is slain by the jealous sons. In <u>Moses and Monotheism</u> Moses is denied a Jewish identity, but instead is a son of the Egyptian nobility, "thus saying unconsciously: 'Just as Moses was not born from humble Jews, I am also not a Jew but a man of royal descent.'"[39]

Due to his protean interests, Freud took eight years to complete medical school, three years more than required. His encyclopedic concerns included philosophy and languages, and other domains of knowledge barely touched upon in the regular curriculum. In time he read Latin and Greek with facility, knew Hebrew, wrote in French and English (as well as in his native German) and corresponded in Italian and Spanish. Ultimately Freud's experiences in the physiology laboratory of Ernst Brücke helped him to focus his interests. He abandoned further intellectual digression and graduated in 1881.

At this time Freud's interests were focused upon medical research and he remained in Brücke's laboratory to study anatomy and physiology. Here a compelling doctrine was espoused.

> The investigation of . . . living organisms required the rejection of any a <u>priori</u> metaphysical system. . . .
> Life was equated with matter and energy . . . to be . . . explained in material terms, that is, in terms of the chemical and physical forces. . . .
> Intention and purpose had no place . . . . This doctrine, combining positivism, mechanism and materialism, was the philosophy to which Freud was exposed . . . as a medical student and young physician.[40]

The Vienna of Freud's young manhood was a city for which Freud often expressed dislike, because of its perceived intellectual sterility. Nevertheless, this environment did much to shape both his early and later thought. At least one source for the rich intellectual well-spring of psychoanalysis

undoubtedly was the ideal of a universally educated man which inspired the curriculum of the Austrian educational system . . . [with] emphasis . . . heavily on the classical languages . . . but natural sciences and mathematics were also taught very thoroughly . . . the examination which gave access to the University . . . had to be taken in humanist and science subjects. Moreover, so powerful was the ideal of universal culture . . . that even those who . . . specialized [in] . . . law and medicine [felt it necessary] to show . . . interest in music, painting and literature.[41]

The supposedly bleak atmosphere of Freud's city in the period near the turn of the nineteenth century

was . . . the crucible of many of the most important ideas which have . . . shaped our century . . . . [In Vienna and its cultural environs were laid] the foundations of logical positivism and linguistic philosophy; . . . Schonberg developed twelve-tone music; Adolph Loos pioneered modern architecture . . . Kafka revolutionized modern literature . . . and Freud created psychoanalysis.[42]

Moreover, Freud typified the Viennese medical man with his wide-ranging interests in the theatre, art, archeology, and literature. "Only a medical man with a deep classical culture could have produced the synthesis of science and symbolical thought which is psychoanalysis."[43]

To return to Freud's early career: After a postgraduate year in Brücke's laboratory Freud left, in 1882, at age twenty-six, in order to earn a more adequate income. He had begun a four-year engagement to a German-Jewish woman, Martha Bernays, and marriage would be impossible, according to prevailing norms, until Freud could independently support a wife and family. Between his twenty-seventh and thirtieth years Freud wrote voluminously to his fiance. The letters portray an ambitious, hard-working, somewhat dogmatic Freud, fervently devoted and jealous.[44] The periods of separation proved too much for Freud on one critical occasion. He left to visit Martha after mentioning to a colleague his preliminary results on the investigation of the properties of cocaine. The colleague took up the work and, by publishing ahead of Freud, received credit for discovery of the use of cocaine as a local anaesthetic. This cost the ambitious Freud an opportunity to augment his reputation.

The marriage to Martha in 1886 was a fruitful union. Six children were born. Though for Freud his work always remained of primary importance, he remained a devoted and faithful husband, and the head of a large entourage. From the summer of 1891 until the fall of 1939, the family lived in an apartment selected by Freud at Bergasse 19, Vienna. The group included husband, wife, six children, Freud's sister-in-law and two or three servants.[45]

Freud's theoretical interests in physiology, anatomy, and the nervous system had to be set aside for the more practical considerations of earning a living, which he proceeded to do as a hospital physician. His interest in brain anatomy led him toward the study of "nervous" diseases. As the recipient of a traveling fellowship for which he had applied in order to work under the famous French neurologist, Charcot, Freud spent the year 1885 in Paris. He became Charcot's favorite pupil, published a number of papers on neuro-physiology, and through Charcot became aware of hypnosis as a therapeutic method for treatment of hysteria. Freud returned to Vienna in 1886, to marry and to enter private practice, armed with this new therapeutic instrument.[46]

Those suffering hysteria constituted a substantial segment of the caseloads of many psychiatrists and were the object of considerable contemporary medical interest. Freud found that hypnotic suggestion seemed effective in suppressing hysterical symptoms. Nevertheless, hypnosis proved a tool of limited utility. Some patients were difficult to hypnotize, others experienced only transitory improvement; moreover, Freud disliked the magical connotations which surrounded the hypnotic state. In quest of an alternative method, Freud joined Joseph Breuer, an older physician who, in addition to using hypnosis as an instrument of recall, encouraged patients to ventilate their feelings. This was the method of catharsis.

In 1893, Breuer and Freud published a paper on hypnosis in the treatment of "nervous" illness. This was followed in 1895 by the book, <u>Studies in Hysteria</u>. This work was of epochal significance. In addition to numerous case histories the work contained the first full statement of a theory of neurosis. The book stressed the importance of the emotional life, and of differentiating between conscious and unconscious mental activity, and introduced a dynamic factor into psychiatry by pointing to symptoms as a consequence of dammed-up forces. Freud now suspected the existence of "powerful mental processes which nevertheless remained hidden from . . . consciousness. . . ."[47] Freud had discovered that mental symptoms were meaningful; they expressed conflict at an unconscious level of the personality. As such they constituted a proper subject for psychological investigation rather than being ignored as random epiphenomena of physical aberration.

The hysterical patients whom Breuer and Freud were treating seemed to Freud to be expressing conflict based upon a sexual etiology. Breuer apparently rejected this idea and the two physician investigators severed their association. Freud then began to investigate the sexual life of his other neurotic patients. He also relinquished altogether the use of hypnosis. He adopted instead what became the "fundamental rule" of psychoanalysis, viz., free association. This was designed to encourage the patient to express, without reflection, all thoughts and feelings which entered consciousness, however trivial, absurd or shocking they might appear to be. The unconsciously associated train of thoughts would inevitably reveal significant areas of conflict for therapeutic intervention.

In time Freud modified his ideas about the role of sexuality in the neuroses. However, his conviction about the central importance of conflict and aggression in the human psyche was strengthened. Later, in his social works, these elements (conflict and aggression) were extrapolated to the level of social institutions and society itself.

Now followed years of a modest practice, barely sufficient to support his family. But the practice grew, as did both publications and fame. During the prime of his life Freud engaged in the daily life of a working physician. Between the hours of 9:00 a.m. and 8:00 p.m. he analyzed as many as ten patients, interrupted only by lunch and a walk break with his wife and daughter. After his last patient Freud dined with the family, then retired to his study, where he wrote, saw friends, and corrected proofs, sometimes to 1:00 a.m. Freud also became a dedicated collector. His desk and consulting room were laden with antiquities.[48] Freud's fascination with the distant past also was reflected in his wide reading in ethnology. He later put this material to use in his social works, most notably in Totem and Taboo and in Moses and Monotheism.

During the period 1896-98 there occurred a productive outpouring seldom, if ever, equalled by one individual: the technique of psychoanalysis, the sexual theory of the neuroses and psychoses, the theory of repression, the theory of infantile sexuality, the doctrine of the Oedipus complex, and the construction of his own theory of the unconscious[49] were conceived and presented.

In 1900 Freud published The Interpretation of Dreams, perhaps his most influential and trail-blazing work, which with Totem and Taboo, he later judged his personal favorites. By the first decade of the twentieth century Freud had published extensively and had propagated psychoanalysis with sufficient success to attract a small but brilliant group of followers. His work also was becoming known beyond local medical circles. In September, 1909, some twenty-six years after his first publication on psychoanalysis, Freud, responding to an invitation, delivered five lectures on psychoanalysis at Clark University. This marked his first and only journey to the United States. On receiving an honorary degree at the conclusion, he commented, "This is the first official recognition of our endeavors." Indeed, his lectures had been received with enthusiasm, and new American disciples were added to the fold. It seems one of the ironies of Freud's life and work that, although he always had a low regard for the United States, the greatest acceptance of his doctrines occurred in this country. Prior to World War II, and during its aftermath, the most productive psychoanalytic workers emigrated to the United States. In contrast with the totalitarian regimes which were antagonistic to psychoanalysis, American empiricism welcomed the new doctrine. By the nineteen fifties New York City had more psychoanalysts than all countries of the world combined.

The first world war brought further support to psychoanalytic concepts by pointing up the psychogenesis of wartime neuroses--even as it disrupted or suspended contacts between psychoanalysts of various countries. Following the war Freud published more of his "speculative" (as contrasted with his clinically based) works, while continuing to elaborate his clinical thought.

Events in the Austria of Freud's later years continued to exert influence on his thinking. With the collapse of the Hapsburg empire in 1918, Vienna entered a period marked by poverty, heightened intellectual controversy, galloping inflation, and renewed impetus to anti-Semitic propaganda, stimulated by a refugee influx from eastern Europe which raised the resident Jewish population to its high point in 1923. The financial ruin of many wealthy families was accompanied by the city's inundation by profiteers, political opportunists, and gangsters. "The deep pessimism of the later Freud about the discontents of civilization should be seen against the background of this profound malaise."[50]

Freud's seventieth birthday in 1926 became an international event. Telegrams and letters of congratulations poured in. Notes arrived from Einstein and other notables; foreign universities sent messages and the freedom of the city of Vienna was conferred upon him In 1930 the Goethe prize for literature was awarded him by the City of Frankfort, as well as honorary memberships in various learned societies.[51]

Freud's eightieth birthday in 1936 produced another flood of congratulations. Einstein wrote Freud indicating his belief in the validity of the theory of repression, based upon a personal experience. Thomas Mann delivered to Freud an essay signed by himself and other leading intellectuals. Meanwhile, however, the reptilian shadow of Nazism had begun to snake its deadly way across central Europe. In 1938, Austria was occupied. The intercession of the British and American governments and the payment

33

of a huge ransom allowed the reluctant Freud, and his family, to leave Vienna for England in June. Here he completed Moses and Monotheism. Bronislaw Malinowski, H. G. Wells, and others visited. Freud, who was now terminally ill with a cancer of the jaw and palate which he had endured stoically since 1923, was steadily weakening. But he remained lucid and continued analyzing four patients a day until the end of July.[52] As the summer passed, Freud grew weaker. He died peacefully in his sleep just before midnight of September 23rd.

Freud's Personality and the Psychoanalytic Movement

Even the great innovators who develop new syntheses also to some extent simply create or recreate the world in their own image. Thus the discoverer also reveals himself. Therefore, it may be instructive to identify some well known facets of Freud's personality and examine the movement he founded. This may contribute some understanding of the sources and directions of Freud's social thought.

It must first be recognized that there appears something inexplicable about the ultimate direction of Freud's thought. A product of training strictly based in an organic model, he developed a theory of personality and human behavior rooted in psychological factors. The hypothesis of genius is therefore a tempting one, i.e., that here appeared an individual of profound and unique gifts who surpassed conventional limits of development. Apart from the fact this "explanation" constrains further exploration, Freud himself would have disparaged it. He noted,

> We know that genius is incomprehensible and unaccountable and it should therefore not be called upon as an explanation until every other solution has failed.[53]

We know that Freud's interests transcended medicine. Jones reported that

> To medicine itself he felt no direct attraction. He did not conceal in later years that he never felt at home in the medical profession, and that he did not seem to himself to be a regular member

of it .... [As early as 1910 Freud wished] with a sigh that he could retire from medical practice and devote himself to the unravelling of cultural and historical problems--ultimately the great problem of how man came to be what he is.⁵⁴

Clearly Freud was interested in the questions which animate philosophy and the social sciences. His social works undertook to unravel the "cultural and historical problems" which intrigued him as much as the problems of the neuroses.

Freud brought to his endeavors tremendous energy and capacity for work, intense concentration on chosen goals, both physical and moral courage. He was a person of scrupulous honesty who admired both Darwin's scientific integrity and his psychological acumen. Freud quoted approvingly from Darwin's autobiography:

'I had during many years, followed a golden rule, namely, that whenever a published fact, a new observation or thought, came across me which was opposed to my general results, to make a memorandum of it without fail and at once; for I had found by experience that such facts and thoughts were far more apt to escape from the memory than favorable ones.'⁵⁵

Freud believed firmly in the work ethic. The world of work was the only significant world. Even on the level of the unconscious one dealt with the "dream work" and the "work of mourning" rather than the world of pleasure. The latter was the world of the child, the immature, the neurotic, the woman, the aristocrat. Maturity meant the ability to work and to love ("lieben und arbeiten"). Freud exemplified a strong sense of duty and great ambition and sometimes a sense of depression when he feared he would not achieve anything noteworthy. From 1900 on his self-assurance grew as his self-analysis and burgeoning reputation convinced him he had made a significant discovery.

Among Freud's outstanding traits must be included his persistent feeling of isolation, which runs like a thread through the texture of his life. Thus, in his autobiography, Freud commented,

35

For more than ten years after my separation from Breuer [c. 1895-96] I had no followers. I was completely isolated. In Vienna I was shunned. . . .[56]

On May 6, 1926, on Freud's seventieth birthday, the Viennese chapter of the Society of B'nai B'rith had honored him. Freud acknowledged in his acceptance address that he had joined this Jewish cultural organization to compensate for the sense of isolation forced by the announcement of his "unpleasing discoveries. . . . I felt as though I were despised and universally shunned."[57]

Freud had the **personality of a Romantic**. Fritz Wittels, a psychoanalyst and a biographer of Freud, commented that the latter was, in a sense, a misplaced person, a contemporary of Bismarkian Germany but belonging to the age of Goethe.[58] Ellenberger agrees.

> In his style of life there was much of Romanticism . . . . It is as though Freud identified himself with the Byronic figure of the lonely hero struggling against a host of enemies and difficulties . . . . The formation of a secret group of six chosen disciples who pledged their allegiance to the defense of psychoanalysis, each of them receiving a ring from Freud, was an eminently Romantic idea. That Freud should suddenly harbor feelings of Austrian patriotism, after a long period of political indifference, when the [first world] war broke out, is reminiscent of the patriotic fervor of the young German Romanticists in 1806. Finally, much in psychoanalysis can be understood as a revival of the . . . philosophy of nature and Romantic medicine.[59]

Whatever the objective data provide, Freud's own perception of his status was that of beleaguered champion, and, as W. I. Thomas pointed out, a situation perceived as real is real in its consequences. The psychoanalytic movement, under Freud's guidance, developed as though it was an entity under siege. There developed an official doctrine,

36

deviation from which courted expulsion from the ranks of the faithful, a rigid organization and hierarchy, specialized journals, a membership closed to all but those willing and able to endure the prolonged initiation (specialized training).

Freud's identification with Judaism was lifelong and was strengthened by recurrent anti-Semitism. It was evident in his preoccupation with the figure of Moses. Freud's personality

> has been strongly shaped by the traditions of his Jewish community. He kept the patriarchal ideology, with its belief in the domination of man and subordination of women, its devotion to the extended family and its . . . puritanical mores. . . . [60]

Freud, regarding males as inherently the superior sex, held therefore, that a man was entitled to control his wife. His translating of John Stuart Mill's writings led him to write Martha (then his fiance):

> It is really a stillborn thought to send women into the struggle for existence exactly as men. . . . [N]ature has determined women's destiny through beauty, charm and sweetness. . . . [T]he position of women [despite changes in law and custom will remain] in youth an adored darling, and in mature years a loved wife.[61]

While these views were characteristic of the middle-class European male of his period, why should they reflect Freud's? He was in many ways in rebellion against conventional beliefs and attitudes. It suggests a profound need to regard women as inferior. His opinion persisted even a half century later. Freud had criticized American culture as matriarchal, and, when asked if it would not be best if the marriage partners were equal, responded,

> That is a practical impossibility. There must be inequality and the superiority of the man is the lesser of two evils.[62]

Fromm asserts that Freud's dependency on his mother was also manifested in his relationship to his wife and

> also to men, older ones, contemporaries and disciples, upon whom he transferred the same need for unconditional love, affection, admiration and protection.[63]

The bitter strife which periodically erupted within the psychoanalytic movement, culminating in the successive defections of such once-favored sons as Adler, Jung, Stekel, and others, now perhaps becomes more understandable, for

> Freud viewed society as naturally and necessarily authoritarian and the family as paternalistic. As he had respected his mentors he expected his followers to respect him.[64]

Moreover, Freud needed absolute and unconditional fealty. His own fierce desire for independence was accompanied by an equally fierce desire to be admired and protected. His relationships with his major adherents followed a sequence of "ardent friendship, confidence, dependence, changing into suspicion and hate."[65]

Freud identified Carl Jung as the Joshua destined to explore the promised land of psychiatry to which Freud was leading his followers. In reporting this remark which had appeared in a letter Freud wrote to Jung, Jones sees it as further confirmation of Freud's self-identification with Moses, "one which in later years became very evident."[66]

Indeed, Freud's drive to achieve heroic stature could not be denied even in the throes of old age, flight from the Nazi terror, and mortal illness. On the boat train from Paris to London he dreamed he was landing at Pevensey, at the site where William the Conqueror had landed in 1066.[67] What a reversal--from refugee to conqueror!

Before 1910 Freud had achieved his most fundamental discoveries, which he reported to physicians and psychologists in the Viennese scientific community. Apparently this was not sufficient for Freud. Between 1910 and 1914 occurred the launching of psychoanalysis as a "movement." It was organized along dictatorial lines, in furtherance of the thought of a leading adherent, Ferenczi, that

> the psychoanalytic outlook does not lead to a democratic equalizing: there should be an elite rather on the lines of Plato's rule of the philosophers.
> [Letter to Freud, Feburary 5, 1910.]

Freud replied that he had already thought the same.[68] There were other indications that Freud (and his followers) saw the International Psychoanalytic Association and its Congresses as more than scientific conclaves. For one thing Freud, over the strenuous opposition of his Viennese Jewish analyst-disciples, insisted that the Swiss analysts be given leadership positions in the organization. This would enhance the latter's acceptance as a world-wide movement. Jung, the most prominent of these non-Jewish followers, "had to become, as it were, the Paul of the new religion."[69]

After the first years of unity, dissension burst forth, with a bitterness that cannot be explained on grounds of theoretical divergence alone. The break with Jung, his putative heir, led to a further tightening of the inner ranks. A secret international committee was formed to watch over the purity of psychoanalytic doctrine and the integrity, i.e., loyalty, of Freud's remaining followers. In On the History of the Psychoanalytic Movement Freud wrote of the "final, decisive battle for psychoanalysis and of the necessity for a 'leader' whose function would be to 'instruct and admonish' and a 'headquarters whose duty it would be to [decide whether new developments conformed to accepted doctrine].'"[70]

The language employed by Freud should be noted. We read of a "decisive battle," a "leader," and "headquarters." The acrid smell of combat is evoked. As will be seen later in discussion of his social works, conflict was central to Freud's view of society and human relationships.

A Summing Up

Sigmund Freud combined in his person a number of charcteristics which were reflected in his thought.

He was a Jew and the firstborn male, heir to a patriarchal, authoritarian family tradition which took male authority and superiority as givens. Freud never doubted his favored status, reinforced as it was by the realities of his privileged family treatment and the overt adoration of his mother. Thus his confidence in his ultimate success in life remained strong. At the same time his Jewish identify in anti-Semitic Vienna and central Europe and the nature of his ideas forced him into the status of marginal man. Whatever the reality of anti-Semitic and other adverse reactions to him and his work (and there is disagreement on this score)[71], such was his perception. To a person of his intelligence, indefatigable ambition, and wide learning this marginality was an asset for it sanctioned boldness, a departure from conventional thought. Innovative ideas in psychological and social thought, described in subsequent chapters, were produced.

At the same time Freud's father was a disappointing role model. Twice the age of his wife, he was a relatively old man when Sigmund was born. He was a reserved person who admired his son's academic brilliance but behaved humiliatingly (in Sigmund's view) when he meekly suffered the contempt of his Gentile tormentor. Freud's need for absolute fealty from his followers (sons) may represent both his belief in the legitimacy of patriarchal authority and his need to assert how his own father should have behaved in the face of threatened status deprivation. Freud's belief in inherent male superiority, the patriarchy, and the legitimacy of the model of the contemporary European middle class family, figures prominently in his social works. Theories of social origins, social groups, the family, and religion, to be discussed in Chapters IV and V, reflect these beliefs.

Sigmund Freud had profound faith in the power of reason. In this respect he was a child of the Enlightenment. Reason was presumed to enable man to overcome life's illusions, including religion; it was the only way to achieve truth and free oneself of irrational beliefs. In this respect Freud belonged among the late nineteenth century intellectuals "who posited their faith in rationalism, in the progress of civilization through the advance of science."[72]

The Jewish heritage extolled reason and intellectual discipline; moreover, a marginal man had compelling reasons to fight against irrationality and superstition as impediments to the achievement of equality.

Granted the authenticity of Freud's faith in reason, his orientation to life appears more complex than this. Freud inherited and initally espoused his era's materialism,

> being wedded to the determinism and the classical physicalism of nineteenth century physiology. . . . But at the same time . . . there was a deep current of romanticism in Freud--a sense of the role of impulse, of the drama of life, of the power of symbolism, of ways of knowing that were more poetic than rational in spirit, of the poet's cultural alienation.[73]

Freud thus embodied two essentially antithetical traditions, those of romanticism and nineteenth century scientism.

Freud probably exaggerated the extent of the opposition his ideas encountered; on the other hand, hostility to his ideas was more than a figment of his imagination.

Above all, Freud sought to be original. As much as possible, he avoided learning what others had done or were doing along lines he was pursuing. To his friend, Fliess, he wrote, "I do not want to read, because it stirs up too many thoughts and stints me of the satisfaction of discovery." (Emphasis added.) Concerning reading, Freud wrote, in another letter, "It is the oldest ideas which are the most useful, as I am finding out." In still another letter he wrote of his discomfiture that "my brand-new theory of the primary origins of hysteria is already familiar. . . . "[74] Freud's need for recognition, even glory, stands in contrast with the attitude of his great contemporary, Georg Simmel. The sociologist wrote in his diary:

> I know that I will die without intellectual heirs--and that is as it

should be. My legacy will be in cash, distributed to many heirs, each transforming his part into use conforming to his own nature: a use that will no longer reveal its indebtedness to this heritage.[75]

Creativity apparently may be found among both the overwhelmingly ambitious and the self-effacing.

In the next chapter will be presented a brief overview of the structure of Freud's clinical thought. This became the source of many of the ideas he extrapolated to the wider world of man's social life. Then will follow summaries of his major social essays.

NOTES

[1] Henri F. Ellenberger, The Discovery of the Unconscious (New York: Basic Books, Inc., 1970), p. 183, 184.

[2] Ibid., p. 198.

[3] Ibid., p. 203.

[4] Ernest Jones, The Life and Work of Sigmund Freud, Vol. II (New York: Basic Books, 1955), 318.

[5] Ellenberger, op. cit., p. 225.

[6] Ellenberger, op. cit., pp. 234, 235.

[7] Ibid., p. 255.

[8] Ibid., p. 271.

[9] Friedrich Nietzsche, Genealogy of Morals, in Walter Kaufmann, The Portable Nietzsche (New York: Viking Press, 1954).

[10] Ellenberger, op. cit., p. 275.

[11] Sigmund Freud, "An Autobiographical Study," in the Standard Edition of the Complete Psychological Works of Sigmund Freud, Vol. XX, (London: The Hogarth Press, 1959), p. 60.

[12] Nietzsche in Kaufmann, op. cit., pp. 117, 146, and 147.

[13] Morton Levitt, Freud and Dewey on the Nature of Man (New York: Philosophical Library, Inc., 1960), p. 3.

[14] A. I. Hallowell, "The Child, The Savage and Human Experience," in Proceedings of the Sixth Institute on the Exceptional Child (Langhorne, Pennsylvania: Child Research Clinic of the Woods Schools, October 1939), pp. 18, 19.

[15] Freud, op. cit., pp. 230, 232, 250.

[16] Gerald N. Izenberg, The Existentialist Critique of Freud (Princeton, New Jersey: Princton University Press, 1976), pp. 24, 25.

[17] Iago Galdston, "Freud and Romantic Medicine," (Bulletin of the History of Medicine, 1956), pp. 498, 499.

[18] Hannah S. Decker, Freud in Germany (New York: International Universities Press, 1977), pp. 27-28.

[19] Ibid., p. 29.

[20] Ibid., p. 30.

[21] Franz Alexander and S. T. Selesnick, The History of Psychiatry: An Evaluation of Psychiatric Thought and Practice From Prehistoric Times to the Present (New York: Harper and Row, 1966), p. 146.

[22] G. Mora, "The Historiography of Psychiatry and Its Development: A Re-evaluation," Journal of the History of Behavioral Science, Vol. 1, 1965, p. 47.

[23] Ernest Jones, The Life and Work of Sigmund Freud, Vol. I (New York: Basic Books, Inc., 1953), p.40.

[24] Gregory Zilboorg, A History of Medical Psychology (New York: Norton, 1941), p. 400.

[25] Decker, op. cit., p. 42.

[26] Ellenberger, op. cit.

[27] Decker, op. cit., p. 258 (footnote).

[28] Ibid., pp. 257, 258.

[29] Ibid., p. 259.

[30] Randall Collins and Michael Makowsky, The Discovery of Society, rev. 2nd ed. (New York: Random House, 1978), p.137.

[31] Lancelot L. Whyte, The Unconscious Before Freud (Garden City, New York: Doubleday Anchor Books, 1962), p. 90.

[32] Freud, op. cit.

[33] Gerard Lauzan, *Sigmund Freud, The Man and His Theories*, trans. by Patrick Evans (Greenwich, Connecticut, Fawcett Publications, Inc., 1965), p. 13.

[34] Sigmund Freud, *Collected Works* (London, Hogarth Press), Vol. 14, 1952, 367.

[35] Lauzan, op. cit., p. 16.

[36] Sigmund Freud, *An Autobiographical Study*, op. cit., p. 11.

[37] Erich Fromm, *Sigmund Freud's Mission* (New York: Harper and Brothers Publishers, 1959), p. 57.

[38] Ibid., p. 57.

[39] Ibid., p.59.

[40] George Rosen, "Freud and Medicine in Vienna," in *Freud, The Man, His World, His Influence*, Jonathan Miller, ed. (Boston: Little, Brown and Company, 1972), p.29.

[41] Martin Esslin, "Freud's Vienna," (Miller), p.46.

[42] Ibid., p. 43.

[43] Ibid., p.46.

[44] Ernst Freud, ed., *Letters of Sigmund Freud*, trans. by Tania and James Stern (New York: Basic Books, Inc., 1960), pp. 7-218.

[45] Ellenberger, op. cit., p. 443.

[46] Ellenberger, op. cit., p. 28.

[47] Sigmund Freud, op. cit., p. 17.

[48] Lauzan, op. cit., pp. 86, 87.

[49] Ernest Jones, "Sigmund Freud," *International Journal of Psychoanalysis*, 1940, 21, pp. 1-26.

[50] Esslin, op. cit., pp. 53-54.

[51] Lauzan, op. cit., p. 104.

[52] Ibid., p. 109.

[53] Sigmund Freud, Moses and Monotheism, trans. by Katherine Jones (New York: Random House, 1939), p. 81.

[54] Jones, The Life and Work of Sigmund Freud, op. cit., Vol. I, p. 27.

[55] Levitt, op. cit., p. 77. (Quoted from Freud's Psychopathology of Everyday Life).

[56] Sigmund Freud, An Autobiographical Study, ibid., p. 48.

[57] James Strachey, ed., Standard Edition of the Complete Psychological Works of Sigmund Freud, trans. by James Strachey and Anna Freud, Vol. XX (London: Hogarth Press, 1959), p. 273.

[58] Fritz Wittels, Freud and His Times (New York: Liveright, 1931), pp. 3-46.

[59] Ellenberger, op. cit., pp. 456-466.

[60] Ibid., p. 427.

[61] Jones, The Life and Work of Sigmund Freud, Vol. I, 177 (Letter to Martha, November 5, 1883).

[62] Joseph Wortis, Fragment of an Analysis with Freud (New York: Simon and Schuster, 1954), p. 98.

[63] Fromm, Sigmund Freud's Mission, op. cit., p. 18.

[64] Ellenberger, op. cit., p. 465.

[65] Fromm, op. cit., p. 54.

[66] Jones, op. cit., Vol. II, p. 33.

[67] Ibid., p. 228.

[68] Letters quoted in Jones, ibid., Vol. II, p. 68.

[69] Fromm, op. cit., p. 86.

[70] Sigmund Freud, Collected Papers, op. cit., Vol. I, p. 316, 329, 330.

[71] Ellenberger, op. cit., pp. 547, 548; Decker, op. cit., p. 324; Ibid., p. 326.

[72] Jacob Arlow, M.D., The Legacy of Sigmund Freud (New York: International Universities Press, Inc., 1956), p. 69.

[73] Jerome S. Bruner, "Freud and the Image of Man" In Freud: Modern Judgments, Frank Cioffi, ed. (London: MacMillan, 1973) pp. 140, 141.

[74] Galdston, op. cit., p. 115.

[75] Thomas S. Szasz, "Freud as a Leader," in Cioffi, op. cit., p. 156.

CHAPTER III

FREUD'S CLINICAL THOUGHT AND SOCIAL WORKS

This chapter provides an overview of Freud's clinical thought, followed by summaries of the major works which will be analyzed for Freud's social thought.

Psychoanalysis, generally regarded as a therapy for the neuroses, also constitutes a research methodology, a theory of human development and behavior, even a philosophy of man. Psychoanalysis grew out of the theory and practice of nineteenth century medicine. This precursor viewed man as a biological organism, mechanical in action and chemical in composition. The structures and processes necessary to life were empirically ascertainable. Pasteur's work in bacteriology had established links between specific diseases and specific causal agents. Definitions of diseases and their etiologies had thus been placed on an objective, organic foundation. Emotions, thoughts, and behavior were viewed as epiphenomena of organic processes, and disturbances of the former must be signs of an objective disease entity. The "person" as a logically distinct entity was not taken into account.

> By the last third of the nineteenth century, psychiatry had been almost completely assimilated to [this] medical outlook . . . . The mentally and emotionally disturbed had come to be seen as 'sick' [because of] organic pathology. . . .
>
> It was because of the 'incomprehensible' and 'incongruous' nature of [mental symptoms] that nineteenth century psychiatry could not afford them status as meaningful behavior and so felt it necessary to . . . reintegrate them

> [T]hey could apparently be explained only by presumed changes in the physical substratum of the psyche. . . . [1]

for mental illnesses were diseases of the brain. Freud came to the study of the neuroses from this general background.

An appreciation may be grasped of how far Freud ultimately deviated from the dominant medical position of his day by reference to a letter written by one DuBois, a collaborator of the famous Helmholtz. The latter enjoyed the distinction of having his name identified with the dominant school of psychology prevalent in German universities during Freud's studies. The letter stated that

> Brücke [Freud's medical school mentor, later his employer] and I pledged a solemn oath to put in power this truth: 'No other force than the common physical chemical ones are active within the organism.' [2]

This was the Enlightenment returned to ascendancy, the reiteration of the thinking of Condorcet, of le Mettrie and Holbach. Cassirer captures its essence with the comment

> All the processes of nature, including those commonly called 'intellectual.' the whole physical and moral order of things, are reducible to matter and motion and are completely explicable in terms of these two concepts. [3]

This philosophy of rationalistic materialism, expressed by le Mettrie, for example, in the notion of the human body as an immense clock, left no room for intention and purpose, the very factors which, for Freud, lay at the root of the neuroses. Freud continued to be fundamentally committed to the principles of causality and determinism. While it might be true, in principle, that psychic processes represented the dependent variable in relation to the physiological, Freud by the turn of the century had given up hope of reducing psychological phenomena to the laws of physics and chemistry. He then undertook the task of explaining psychological phenomena in psychological terms. This was an achievement of the first order, contradicting all the prevailing conventional wisdom in psychiatry. Freud's psychodynamic approach offered a major alternative to the organic concept of causality of mental illness. The documentation of unconscious motivation, and of the significance of early childhood experiences, the representation of the personality in conflict with itself and in struggle with the constraints of the environment represented a clean break with a long psychiatric tradition.

Indeed, Galdston, a noted historian of medicine, believes that Freud's break with Breuer centered not, as is generally believed, on the issue of the sexual etiology of hysteria, but on a broad philosophical issue which he says Freud identified in his Autobiographical Study. Breuer advocated a physiological theory of mental pathogenesis, Freud a psychological one. Freud suspected the operation of

> 'intentions and purposes such as are to be observed in normal life.' It was the thwart and repression of such intentions and purposes that . . . proved pathogenic. If one but granted that premise, it was incontrovertible that in our society the intentions and purposes of sexuality were subject to the greatest thwart and repression. But the premise was not granted, either by Breuer or by the world of Science.[4]

Why, asks Galdston, was the premise rejected? Because

> the imputation of life and . . . its . . . phenomena of intention and purpose was anathema to all the 'best brains' in biology and medicine. Intentions and purposes smacked of vitalism, and reeked of teleology. Life, according to prevailing scientific belief, was to be accounted for in terms of matter and energy, in terms of molecules in motion. Purpose and intention had neither place nor meaning in the realm of science. Yet Freud postulated not molecules and motion but intention and purpose--'such,' he added, 'as are to be observed in normal life.'[5]

51

Although Freud achieved this conceptual breakthrough, the influence of the strongly deterministic and positivistic philosophy of the nineteenth century, which regarded the human organism as a complex energy system, left its impression. Thus his models and language were taken from the physical science and mechanics of his time. His system employed the terminology of "forces" and "resistances." Physical scientists believed that energy must be defined in relation to the work it performed. Because the phenomena interesting Freud were of a psychological nature he adopted the term "psychic energy."

Freud was occupied with constructing a framework to explain the evolution, structure, and functions of the psychic apparatus. The latter provided the form and organization with which to process, contain, and direct the energies (libido) of the system. Personality was viewed as a behavioral dynamism, and, in analogy with the first law of thermodynamics which states that matter/energy is indestructible, psychic energy which apparently disappeared actually became converted or transformed, to assert itself in other guises. The human libido contained a relatively fixed quantity of energy available in furtherance of the sexual drive, later to be broadened by Freud to include all life-sustaining drives (Eros). Force-resistance models, as has been indicated, are of nineteenth century origin. However, the conception survives in more current form in such formulations as the stress-adaptation syndrome, conflict theory, and some theories of social change.

Freud introduced order into the mental universe, insisting that this universe operated in accordance with law. The principle of psychic determinism meant that nothing in mental functioning happens by chance. What a person feels, thinks, fantasies, dreams, does, is motivated. This is true in trivial instances--the choice of dessert, and in momentous ones--the choice of a mate. Each has psychic determinants.

Some of these determinants escape casual recognition because they are not part of conscious cognition. They are generated as un-conscious processes. Freud thus made more explicable the fact that people may remain in situations they complain about (e.g., an "unhappy" marriage; a "frustrating" job). People had more to do with arranging their own fates than they might wish to believe.

Both Freud and his great younger contemporary, George Herbert Mead, concerned themselves with the development of "mind." Both recognized mind as a social product. Self-consciousness originated within a social context. Mead's theory of the self posited the individual's development of a sense of others' responses, of their reactions to the person's own actions; in time these responses were consolidated into a "generalized other." The latter represented the attitudes of the social group and helped both to orient the person to social expectations and, through the person's responses to the generalized other, provide a sense of individual identity.

Mead's self consisted of an "I" and a "me." The former, conceptualized as the spontaneous, subjective, uniquely individual and action-initiating component of the self, left room for a self not bound by social constraints. The me comprised the objective, cooperative, conventional self, the product of the incorporated generalized other.

Freud used three components to Mead's two. His structural theory of the mind hypothesized, as Freud represented them in German, das Es (literally, the "It"), das Ich (the "I"), and das Über-Ich (the "Super-I"). The Latin rendition, id, and the terms ego, and superego invariably are used in English translations of Freud's works thus obscuring, as Philip Rieff[6] points out, the straightforward nature of these terms. The id chronologically and in terms of depth is the most primitive part of the mind. At birth id is co-extensive with the unconscious, all mental processes being on that level. The id represents innate drives which seek gratification: attainment of pleasure or the relief of tension, and avoidance of pain. (This comes very close to echoing Bentham's formulation, "Nature has placed mankind under the governance of two sovereign masters, Pain and Pleasure.") The id knows no scruples or restraints but is entirely a creature of impulse.

But reality shapes other outcomes. As the infant's sensory apparatus matures and experience with the outside world accrues, consciousness develops, and with it experience and reason, in order to accommodate to, and deal with the world of reality. This second, "higher organ" of the mind mediates between the inner world of id drives, and societal constraints and other impinging realities. Cognition, perception, rational thought, judgement, reality testing, are ego functions.

There exists yet a third force, the superego, which serves as society's internalized representative. Acquired largely through inter-personal experiences leading to incorporation of parental strictures and permissions, it provides the guiding "rights" and "wrongs," the "oughts" and "ought-nots" which inhibit impulse and channel behavior into socially approved paths. The id and superego thus confront each other in fundamental and ceaseless opposition, with the ego serving as arbiter. Freud thus hypothesizes a self in conflict with itself, influenced by the active, if unconscious operation of the internalized social norms. This view of the individual in a dynamic state of conflict, has had compelling resonance, says Rieff.

> No small part of Freud's impact upon the contemporary moral imagination derives from his idea of the self in conflict. He conceives of the self not as an abstract entity, uniting experience and cognition, but as the subject of a struggle between two objective forces--unregenerate instincts and overbearing culture. Between these two forces there may be compromise but no resolution. . . . [for] the individual can neither extirpate his instincts nor wholly reject the demands of society.[7]

The need to repress unacceptable impulses makes the person aware of the existence of a world outside the self. This consciousness gives us also the sense of self. Thus the Freudian theory of the self requires society. Consciousness of the self is built upon the repressions originating in the normative structure. In incorporating society a self also is acquired.

Everything about the human organism which is social stems from the need for external "objects." The latter are necessary for "instinctual" gratifications, and drive attainment becomes a major goal of the organism. The organism's drives have four characteristics: a $\underline{source}$, in a bodily condition or need, e. g., hunger or sex; an $\underline{aim}$, that of release of tension, or achievement of pleasure; an $\underline{object}$, on which the drive is focused, such as food or a person; and an $\underline{impetus}$, whose strength is determined by the force or intensity of the underlying need. This varies from individual to individual and in the same individual from time to time, depending upon circumstances.

The term "drive," as used here, is a translation of the German, Trieb. The customary English translation of this word, as used by Freud, has been "instinct." Thus translated, a perhaps unwarranted additional emphasis is added to Freud's presumed physiological bias. It is difficult to see why translators have so consistently employed the term instinct for the German, Trieb. The authoritative Cassell's German Dictionary offers as English equivalents of Trieb these words, in the following order: ". . . Driving force, motive power; impetus, urge, spur; instinct, impulse, bent, propensity, inclination, desire, liking. . . . "[8] Freud, a scientist and linguist of the first order, could hardly have been unaware both of Trieb's preferred meanings and of the fact there was a perfectly good German word to use if one wished to say "instinct;" the German word is Instinkt.[9]

In any case, Freud did not doubt that a substratum of physiological tensions existed, or was generated in the individual, and that the latter's wishes were the psychic representatives of these bodily tensions. Drives were "observable" as fantasies or wishes. Their gratification reduced tension. But gratification was not always immediately or directly possible because of internal (superego) prohibitions or external (reality) constraints. Some impulses, therefore, were dangerous to the individual's psychic equilibrium and threatening to the ego. To deal with these the ego develops a variety of defenses. These are activated whenever the ego perceives an impulse or a situation which will create internal conflict, or threaten a breakthrough into consciousness of forbidden wishes. The ego's response is to experience anxiety. The latter signals impending danger. The defenses ward off the danger and allay the anxiety. A primary defense is "repression." Psychic energy is employed to bar from consciousness or, alternatively, push out of conscious awareness, knowledge of the dangerous impulse. A number of other defense "mechanisms" were identified by Freud. One of these is "sublimation." The ego's use of sublimation is of interest in connection with this study. Sublimation involves transforming an unacceptable impulse (classically of a sexual nature) into some socially acceptable form which may then be expressed. There is at least an implied recognition that social norms play a significant role in determining the form of expression of inner drives. Psychic conflicts are at least in part a function of developments in a specific culture; the latter's configuration determines which impulses are "natural" and acceptable, and in which forms they may be gratified.

For his clinical work alone, social scientists owe Sigmund Freud a substantial debt. Briefly enumerated the contributions from this facet of his work, include:

1. Psychological phenomena can and should be accounted for in psychological (rather than physiological) terms.

2. Human behavior is invariably meaningful. It is as lawful as the movement of celestial bodies or subatomic particles.

3. The early years of life merit systematic and careful study because of their importance for personality formation and functioning.

4. Human sexuality has been documented as a powerful drive, a basic motivational force, the manifestations of which first appear in early childhood.

5. The existence of another "layer" of mind, of mental processes operating outside of conscious awareness has been documented. These processes influence behavior and exist in apposition and opposition to the external, socially created reality.

6. Observation established many of the ways in which products of unconscious processes (impulses) achieved behavioral and cognitive expression. Documentation of the ego's creation of defense mechanisms opened a major area of study: social psychology.

7. Scientific thought was infused with a conception of human mental activity as characteristically experiencing inner conflict. This, and the related concept of

ambivalence, proved of particular value in relation to social psychologists' conception of thought as the internalization of the social process.

8. "Normal" and "abnormal" mentation and behavior could now be recognized as existing on a continuum. They were not discrete entities; rather, they differed in degree. Moreover, the "abnormal" was a fit object of scientific study.

[P]sychoanalysis has forced [psychology] to admit the structural identity of the normal and the abnormal, and has reduced psychopathology to a disturbance of psychic function; . . . ' by the single assumption of psychic determinism Freud brought every manifestation of the irrational into the sphere of scientific investigation. . . . Sane or insane . . . genius or idiot, . . . sick or healthy, the individual's projections or the projections of social groups are scientific facts capable of being interpreted.'[10]

The works of Freud to be examined for their social thought will now be outlined. Totem and Taboo, published in 1912-1913, deals with Freud's conception of the origins of human society and culture. Mankind existed originally in small hordes, each dominated by an autocratic old male who denied the younger males access to the females. The young sons banded together, killed the old man, and ate him in a communal meal. Inevitably they realized that access to the females on the part of any of them, for the sake of which they had killed the old man, would precipitate a recurrence of the jealousy and killing. This realization, and the joint sense of guilt generated by their patricidal act, caused the brothers to renounce their claims to their mothers and sisters and to band together as a clan, the first real group.

To commemorate the circumstances of their union, the sons periodically undertook a ceremony marked by killing and eating an animal set aside as symbolic of (i.e., equivalent to, in the unconscious) the old man. At all other than the ceremonial occasions this animal was sacred or taboo, i.e., not to be killed or eaten.

Thus were established the two taboos of totemism, viz., exogamy and the sparing of the totem animal. These renunciations constituted the first moral act and lie at the root of all morality, for morality stems from a sense of guilt, and all sense of guilt originates with this initial parricidal act.

Group Psychology and the Analysis of the Ego was published in 1921. Freud returned to the theme of the primal horde. The leader is a representative of the primal father, the group ideal which governs the individual's ego. The group is enamored of authority, has a "thirst for obedience" in Le Bon's phrase. An erotic tie exists between group members analogous to that which binds hypnotist and subject, and regressive behavior is inevitable because in the crowd the individual's ego weakens and his superego (conscience) is replaced by the judgement of the crowd, and particularly its leader. Suggestion exercises a compelling force because of the phenomenon of identification.

Freud discusses group feeling from four aspects: group feeling as a reaction formation against previous sibling jealousy, group feeling as a sublimation of homosexual components of the sexual "instinct," group feeling as it compares with love and hypnosis, and the persistence of aggression in the face of group feeling.

The Future of an Illusion appeared in 1927. Freud now explored the functions of religion as an outgrowth of culture. Culture developed in response to two activities. There were activities directed toward achieving mastery over nature and other activities directed toward regulating human relationships. Every culture's existence required that men work, without regard to subjective satisfactions, and that men renounce some instinctual gratifications. To wring some meaning from a world of hardship and sacrifice, men created fatherly gods. By serving god unstintingly one gained an ally against relentless nature, and, in due course, renunciation of earthly pleasures would be rewarded. Religion served to explain and justify life's travail.

By every reasonable standard, religion was an illusion, incomparably inferior to science as a means of apprehending reality. While it was impossible to forecast what the decline of traditional religion would mean to mankind, nevertheless men needed to be educated for reality, to learn the ways of science so they could recognize in a rational way those laws of their culture which were useful and should be followed, as well as learning the necessity of renunciation in the interests of civilization.

Civilization and its Discontents was originally published in 1929 and 1930. In it Freud develops the theme of the inevitable conflict between the individual's demands for freedom and self-expression and the restrictive demands of society. Civilization can exist only through man's renunciation of certain of his inner drives, specifically those of aggression and self-aggrandizement. Culture serves to inhibit man's destructive drives. Freud suggested that in every individual two trends compete with each other; the one directed toward personal happiness is opposed by that toward unity with the rest of mankind.

All human emotions and interpersonal relationships are ambivalent, i.e., feelings of love and concern invariably are accompanied by feelings of hate and aggression. Human groups provide avenues for projection of hostile and aggressive impulses onto others. The study of a given civilization is the study of how it accommodates and finds expression for those impulses which on the personal level are asocial or anti-social. In civilization, men find protection against their own and others' hostile impulses. In compensation, pleasures must be renounced. Unhappiness, therefore, is an inevitable accompaniment of the development of civilization. This unhappiness stems both from necessary self-denial and an ever-growing sense of guilt which is the inevitable outgrowth of the ambivalence men feel between their love and destructive (divisive) impulses.

Moses and Monotheism, Freud's last book, appeared in 1939. Freud cited evidence indicating that Moses, the greatest figure in Jewish history, was in fact an Egyptian, and probably a leader who preached worship of a single God. He led an exodus of some of the Jewish people from Egypt. This may have been done in hopes of preserving his monotheistic faith.

Moses' followers rebelled against his authority and, in an act reminiscent of the killing of the primal father described in Totem and Taboo, murdered their leader. Ultimately the descendants of those who slew Moses joined with other Jews, adherents of a more primitive faith, and established a new religion. Their monotheism represented an effort to repent their crime against their ancient leader (father) by exalting him above all others. The stress on spirituality and the emphasis on the intellect induced by the Jewish relinquishing of images, and the feeling of righteousness engendered by the renouncing of instinctual pleasures, produced both individual self-confidence and the group conviction of being God's chosen people. To these factors may be attributed the Jews' intellectual eminence and survival in the face of persecution.

In the following two chapters various aspects of Freud's social thought will be considered.

NOTES

[1] Gerald N. Izenberg, The Existentialist Critique of Freud (Princeton, New Jersey: Princeton University Press, 1976), pp. 24,25.

[2] S. Bernfeld, "Freud's Earliest Theories and The School of Helmholtz," Psychoanalytic Quarterly, XIII, July 1944, p. 360.

[3] Ernst Cassirer, The Philosophy of the Enlightenment, trans. by Fritz Koelln and James P. Pettegrove (Princeton, New Jersey: Princeton University Press, 1951), p. 65.

[4] Iago Galdston, "Freud and Romantic Medicine," in Freud: Modern Judgements, Frank Cioffi, ed. (London: MacMillan, 1973), p. 107.

[5] Ibid., p. 108.

[6] Philip Rieff, Freud: The Mind of the Moralist (New York: The Viking Press, 1959), p. 60 (footnote).

[7] Ibid., p. 28.

[8] The New Cassell's German Dictionary, Harold D. Betteridge, ed. (New York: Funk and Wagnalls, 1971), p. 477.

[9] Ibid., p. 246.

[10] Gerard Lauzan, Sigmund Freud, The Man and His Theories, trans. by Patrick Evans (Greenwich, Connecticut: Fawcett Publications, Inc., 1965), pp. 143, 144.

CHAPTER IV

SOCIETY: SOCIAL ORIGINS, SOCIAL CONTROL, AND SOCIAL CHANGE

This chapter presents and analyzes Freud's ideas concerning the development of society[1] and the dynamisms of social control and social change. In the writings of Freud which this study analyzes propositions dealing with macro-social processes are largely implicit. Formulating them in explicit form yields the following summary statements of his views:

1. Among the original human hordes (small groups dominated by a strong, older male), acts of parricide, and resultant guilt, spurred the reconstituting of group life. This stimulated development of a moral sense among humans, which led to the development of civilization.

2. The development of the individual and the development of civilization follow analogous paths.

3. Human inheritance of acquired traits and customs helps perpetuate society and the prevailing social arrangements.

4. Societies achieved order and stability through a social contract.

5. Society's cohesive forces originated from survival needs and erotic drives. (As will be developed subsequently, Freud qualified his position about the role of erotic drives.)

6. Societies inevitably develop hierarchical structures. Stratification results from inherent qualitative differences between individuals.

7. Civilization's development required the denial or sacrifice of basic human satisfactions or happiness-- and this burden continues to grow.

8. A fundamental and irreconcilable conflict exists between society and the individual.

9. The ceaseless sacrifices society requires of mankind, i.e., restraint of sexual freedom and curbing of innate aggressive drives, continually threaten society with disintegration.

10. The historical process reflects the influence of great men. Their superiority of intellect and capacity for sublimation of libidinal and aggressive drives are essential to social order and progress.

Social Origins and Social Control

Civilization begins, says Freud, "with the first attempts to regulate social relationships."[2] This almost banal remark bears no hint of Freud's audacious intent: to reconstruct the very origins of society. First fully elaborated in Totem and Taboo and recapitulated in his last work, Moses and Monotheism, Freud also referred to the theme of social origins in others of his major works cited in this study. Freud acknowledged the priority of Darwin[3] in The Descent of Man (and other writers), who espoused the idea that man lived originally in small groups ("hordes") ruled by an autocratic old man. The horde consisted of the ruler's wives, daughters, and sons. The despot allowed the sons no access to females. This "explained" how inbreeding was kept at a biologically desirable minimum, for the young sons were forced to find wives by abducting them from other hordes. A further supposition held that ultimately the exiled sons united and killed the old man.

Freud modified the latter idea to include the eating of the murdered father in a communal meal. This feast celebrated man's first collective enterprise. The ceremony was stimulated as well by a shared sense of guilt. This, and the realization that attempts to reestablish a sexual monopoly through the primacy of a new ruler would lead to recurrence of jealousy and killing, caused renunciation of claims to the women of their own horde. Now an enduring brotherly bond, based upon common guilt celebrated in the communal meal, established the first lasting group, the clan.

From then on the brothers sought wives from outside their group and they continued to commemorate the parricidal act through a ceremonial slaying and devouring of a symbolic representation of the father. This was the totem animal, which on all but sacred occasions was immune from slaughter or eating, that is, taboo. Morality had been created through their remorseful renunciation of the women of their original group. This was a morality of guilt. Hence, society was constructed upon a resolution of the males' ambivalence toward the despotic patriarch.

The attachments hypothesized to have developed between the brothers in the period following their group parricide

> led at last to a union among them, a sort of social contract. Thus there came into being the first form of a social organization accompanied by a renunciation of instinctual gratification; recognition of mutual obligations; institutions declared sacred, which could not be broken--in short, the beginnings of morality and law. Each renounced the ideal of gaining for himself the position of father, of possessing his mother or sister. With this the taboo of incest and the law of exogamy came into being.[4]

In this passage from Moses and Monotheism Freud has enunciated a social contract theory of social origins based upon a primarily suppressive function: to curb men's sexual and aggressive drives. Moreover, life in communities became possible only when men substituted their combined strength in place of individual domination. This is decisive for civilized existence. Freud's master hypothesis, then, purports to explain not only the origin of society, but of religion, law, totemism, the incest taboo and exogamy, ritual and myths. Brown comments succinctly,

> Law curbs the sexual and aggressive drives, religion, myth and ritual

commemorate the [parricidal] crime and assuage guilt, and society is the overall mechanism of control.[5]

It should be noted that Freud's version of the social contract differs from Hobbes'. The English thinkers's "war of everyone against everyone" culminated in men uniting and delegating their rights to a sovereign. This ruler exercised his power for the good of all. Freud's account might be used to support nullification of absolutism and the divine right of kings. Other differences between the two thinkers will be noted later.

While, in Freud's view, all social relations are coercive, a significant difference exists between the coercions of civilization and the domination of natural forces. In the latter instance control emanates from an external source. But the guilt felt by the brothers following their primal crime became internalized. Thus, the subsequent imposition of authority was not truly a renewal of the original despotism. Instead, the evolved taboos were self-imposed, and repressions generated to serve the needs of the group initiated civilization.

Freud found in primitive societies a model for the repressive character of all societies. In <u>Totem and Taboo</u> repression is manifested in the form of taboos and avoidances. This mode of social control represents the prototype of the "moral and conventional prohibitions by which we ourselves are governed."[6] This conception may be likened to Durkheim's use of anthropological data to develop his own thesis about social control. Durkheim, too, emphasized how primitive societies oriented the individual to the social. However, where Durkheim postulated among primitives a collective consciousness which leads in time to individuation, Freud believed that beneath all types of group consciousness could be found the individual, against whom society exercises the same restrictive influences regardless of the era in question. And the power of taboo in itself demonstrated the ineradicable human drive toward anarchy. Society must be suppressive to contain human rebellion.

Freud was aware that expediency and mutual gain also were implicated in social cohesion. But these factors could not suffice, for they dealt with the issue in terms of rational calculation and implied that social solidarity would endure beyond the concurrence of interests. Freud averred that the essential power which held a group together consisted of libidinal ties, a manifestation of "Eros, which holds together everything in the world."[7] Freud's solution offered an alternative to the Marxist view of society which has stressed economic interest and political expediency. Thus, Freud stressed affective ties between humans as the basic element which led to the social construction of enduring human groups. Marx, on the other hand, took existing social relationships as the source from which affective relationships (ideologies, in his term) were generated. While Marx's position is much closer to the sociological perspective Freud's has the merit of implicating actors in the development of social cohesion. Cohesion ultimately is a human act, embodying both the impersonal forces Marx described and the internal ones with which Freud was concerned. Further treatment of the relationship between Freudian and Marxist thought appears in Chapter VI.

Freud found the development of society and of the individual indissolubly linked. This idea has sociological roots as well. Cooley's assertion that self and society are created simultaneously says the same thing. Evolution of human societies occurred as the pleasure principle (untrammeled gratification of impulses and desires) was replaced by the reality principle (adherence to the constraints of the external world). The identical progression occurred in individual development. This sequence

> recurs throughout the history of mankind and of every individual. Phylogenetically, it occurs first in the primal horde, when the primal father monopolizes power and pleasure and enforces renunciation on the part of the sons. Ontogenetically, it occurs during the period of early childhood. . . . [8]

How could the original deed explain guilt in successive generations which had not participated in the original parricide? Freud wrote that neurotics, like primitive peoples, produced taboos against their own hostile impulses because they "have inherited an archaic constitution as an atavistic vestige.. . ."[9] But the masses, too, were subject to a predisposing influence, for the repeated early acts of parricide and the ensuing intense feelings of guilt meant persistence of the original guilt and the morality they had created.

> [T]he assumption of a collective mind . . . makes it possible to neglect the interruptions of mental acts caused by the extinction of the individual. . . . psychical processes [are] continued from one generation to another. . . . [H]ow much can we attribute to psychical continuity in the sequence of generations? . . . I shall not pretend that these problems are sufficiently explained or that direct communication and tradition . . . are enough to account for the process. . . . A part of the problem [of continuity in the mental life of successive generations] seems to be met by the inheritance of psychical dispositions which, however, need to be given some sort of impetus in the life of the individual before they can be roused into actual operation.[10]

A few critical comments about Freud's views on social origins and social control conclude this section. Freud's account of the replacement of the primal horde by the victorious sons, who formed a new union made possible through an act of renunciation, has already been outlined in the quotation from <u>Moses and Monotheism</u> on page 65. However, even as an allegory (and Freud vacillated on the question of its allegorical nature, as will be discussed in Chapter VI), this explanation of social origins is conceptually deficient, for it begs the question in an important particular. As with Hobbes' social contract theory, the "explanation" assumes what cannot be assumed. What is not explained is how the transition occurred from a situation in which force ruled relationships to one in which socially established norms and institutions regulated human behavior. Guilt, the establishment of taboos, followed by the making of a social contract is a sequence which presupposes the prior existence and operation of the very norms and social institutions they are designed to explain.

Guilt is a reaction to the breach of an existing norm. Something is tabooed as an outcome of already legitimated institutional arrangements. A social contract can only be entered into when existing social relationships sanction the creation and fulfillment of promises and agreements. The presumed primal state can hardly exist a priori, but must logically follow the creation of the social bond. It might be more reasonable to account for any submission to a primal father on utilitarian grounds. The father simply was stronger.

Other difficulties are apparent. Freud subscribed to a variety of Lamarckism, the belief viable in nineteenth century biology but now discredited, that acquired characteristics were inheritable. Evidence for this is completely lacking, as are contemporary anthropological data to substantiate the authorities (Frazer, Lang, Atkinson, etc.) upon whose ethnological works Freud relied when he postulated a primal horde.

Social Reality and Social Cohesion

The hard-won gains of civilization emerged from the act of parricide for which the original band of brothers paid the price of guilt and instinctual renunciation. Continued social cohesion depended upon a hereditary disposition toward instinctual renunciation. Indeed, said Freud, "the degree of instinctual repressions [is] a measure of the level of civilization that has been reached. . . ." [11] However, an important development in Freud's thinking on the sources of repression had occurred by the time Freud,

> after making a long detour through the natural sciences, medicine and psychotherapy, returned to the cultural problems which had fascinated me long before, when I was a youth. . . . [12]

In his earlier clinical writings Freud had postulated an organically determined repression of sexuality paving the way to civilization.[13] Man's adoption of an upright carriage and replacement of smell by sight as the dominant sense were implicated in this repression. Upright posture now exposed the female genitalia to view and would have led to a perpetual state of male arousal; hence repression was necessary to dampen the sexual impulse. This idea is both highly speculative and rather naive in its view of human sexual arousal as an essentially physical phenomenon activated by a single sense, that of sight. In later writings, beginning with The Future of an Illusion in 1927, and highlighted in Civilization and its Discontents, Freud drew upon his insights derived from studies in ego psychology and shifted to an externally operative source of repression. Operation of the reality principle thus again was evidenced.[14] External reality exerted its influence through men's superegos, which had their origin in each individual's earliest object-relations. As Freud developed his thesis about the functioning of society, cohesion thus was grounded upon both external and internal sources.

Inevitably, Freud's interest in the making and maintenance of society prompted his attention to the social construction of reality. His thought maintained its characteristic orientation to the individual, for he viewed society as the individual writ large.

> The projection outward of internal perceptions is a primitive mechanism, to which, for instance, our sense perceptions are subject, and which therefore normally plays a very large part in determining the form taken by our external world. Under conditions whose nature has not yet been sufficiently established, internal perceptions of emotional and thought processes can be projected outwards in the same way as sense perceptions; they are thus employed for building up the external world. . . .[15]

Here Freud reverses Cooley. According to the latter, the sense of individual identity is acquired from interaction with others. However, in the passage above Freud seems to suggest that the external world is defined through some kind of innate perceptual process. This is characteristic of stage theorists in psychology, from Freud to Erikson and Piaget. They postulate a preprogrammed matuational process which then impinges upon the environment. For instance, in discussing cognitive development, Piaget holds with Hamlet that "The [inner] readiness is all." This is not to say that the environment is of no consequence but rather that the construction of reality originates with certain innate givens. Here the divergence of psychological and sociological perspectives appears quite clearly.

In another context Freud rooted the social in the individual by remarking that

> [Our] possibilities of happiness are . . . restricted by our constitution. . . . [The] attempt to procure . . . happiness and a protection against suffering through a delusional remolding of reality is made by a considerable number of people in common.[16]

Freud identified three sources of human suffering.

> We are threatened with suffering from three directions: from our body, which is doomed to decay and dissolution . . . ; from the external world, which may rage against us with overwhelming and merciless forces of destruction; and finally from our relations to other men. The suffering which comes from this source is perhaps more painful to us than any other. . . . Here too a piece of unconquerable nature may lie behind [the failure to achieve satisfying social relationships]--this time a piece of our own psychical constitution. . . .
>
> It is no wonder if, under the pressure of [such] suffering, men . . . moderate their claims to happiness--just as the pleasure principle itself, indeed under the influence of the external world, changed into the more modest reality principle. . . . [17]

Here Freud once again expressed his conviction that civilized society exacts a price in denial of human satisfactions, which themselves are rooted in individual constitutional needs.

When Freud spoke of people's "remodeling of reality" he seemed to open the door to the social construction of reality. But then he reverted to a familiar axiomatic position--man's innate constitution denies him the possibilities of happiness. Thus he failed to recognize that man, in interaction with others, creates and modifies both the conditions of his existence and the definition of what constitutes human happiness. He did see the external world as moderating individual behavior by influencing the transformation from pleasure principle to reality principle. However, to say that civilization, as such, denies human satisfactions generalizes human societies as necessarily repressive without regard to man as an active agent in the construction of that civilization. Even if Freud had been familiar with Mead's work on symbolic interactionism, and there is no evidence he was, it appears unlikely he would have taken seriously Mead's essentially cognitive approach to human relationships.

Freud had yet another idea concerning how men could attain a grasp of reality, which had the further merit of binding them to the human community.

> No other technique for the conduct of life attaches the individual so firmly to reality as . . . work; for his work at least gives him a secure place in a portion of reality, in the human community.[18]

Freud perceptively cited work's value for displacing self-aggrandizing, aggressive and erotic drives. This was as valuable as its material benefits. He could not refrain from adding that men were not made happy by their labors.

> The great majority . . . only work under . . . necessity, and this natural aversion . . . raises most difficult social problems.[19]

Freud's assessment of the significance of work appears in sharp contrast with that of Durkheim. Both recognized the importance of work for personal attachment and social solidarity. However, Durkheim stressed the web of interdependence thus created--an organic solidarity--which made work a preeminently social act; Freud's view of work as a means for displacement of inner drives of a potentially divisive charcter made work a psychologically motivated act whose social consequences were a secondary phenomenon.

If work could not help men achieve social solidarity, there were other factors. For example, an impelling motivation, "the prohibition of incest [had] a powerful practical basis,"[20] i.e., the avoidance of divisive rivalries. Thereby impetus to social organization was provided. This appears to support the idea of a <u>collective</u> act of behavioral restraint. Nevertheless, <u>a dualism</u> permeated Freud's social thought: individual motives appear alongside, and often in opposition to, social factors. Even the forces which supported social coalesence were of individual derivation.

> I took as my starting point a saying . . . that 'hunger and love are what moves the world.' Hunger could be taken to represent the instincts which aim at preserving the individual; while love strives after objects, and its chief function, favoured in every way by nature, is the preservation of the species. Thus . . . ego-instincts and object-instincts confronted each other. . . . Thus the antithesis was between the ego-instincts and the 'libidinal' instincts of love (in its widest sense) which were directed to an object.[21]

Collective behavior also has a strongly utilitarian or functional cast.

> . . . we assume quite generally that the motive force of all human activities is a striving towards the two confluent goals of utility and a yield of pleasure [and] we must suppose that this is also true of the manifestations of civilization.[22]

The Freudian theme of the essentially coercive nature of society is well represented in the following passage. This reference is liberally sprinkled with such terms as "stronger," "united against," "opposition," "sacrifice," "restriction," and "force."

> Human life in common is only made possible when a majority comes together which is stronger than any separate individual and which remains united against all separate individuals. The

power of this community is then set up as 'right' in opposition to the power of the individual, which is condemned as 'brute force.' This replacement of the power of the individual by the power of a community constitutes the decisive step of civilization. The essence of it lies in the fact that the members of the community restrict themselves in their possibilities of satisfaction, whereas the individual knew no such restrictions. . . . The final outcome should be a rule of law to which all . . . have contributed by a sacrifice of their instincts, and which leaves no one . . . at the mercy of brute force.[23]

In a passage which manages to leap the chasm separating Rousseau and Hobbes as contract theorists, Freud comments grimly,

The liberty of the individual is no gift of civilization. It was greatest before there was any civilization, though then . . . it had . . . no value, since the individual was scarcely in a position to defend it. The development of civilization imposes restrictions on it . . . .[24]

It may be that Freud's prolonged immersion in the treatment of human pathology left him with a sense of frustration concerning man's ability to surmount his libidinal drives. Man as host to contending inner forces became his model for man in conflict in his social relationships. There was no recourse but to sacrifice his happiness for the sake of survival.

Thus mankind struggles to accommodate, somehow, the individual's aspirations for happiness and the compelling cultural claims of the group. Freud asks, but does not directly answer, the question whether some particular form of civilization could achieve this accommodation, or whether this is an irreconcilable problem. He considers briefly, and tersely dismisses, the potential benefit of a reordering of the social system along Marxist lines. "Aggressiveness was not created by property."[25]

Upon what, then does social cohesion rest? Freud identified a number of sources. Some of these were "positive" in nature for they emanated from human capacities for cultural achievement; others were "negative" in that they exploited men's weaknesses and inadequacies. Some sources represented practical responses to practical needs; others originated with memory traces inherited from the dawn of mankind's emergence into civilization. Thus, in one formulation Freud viewed social cohesion as stemming from the common guilt of the original act of parricide combined with the need for self-preservation which required restraining of the sexual and aggressive drives. In addition, there were aim-inhibited[26] libidinal ties between members of society based upon their common identification with a leader. Freud thus underscored Max Weber's ideas concerning the cohesive significance of a shared belief in the leader's legitimacy and the power of his charisma. More will be said further on concerning Freud's thought about the role of the leader.

A number of times Freud reiterated his conviction concerning these twin pillars of cohesion: compulsion and ties of sentiment. When Albert Einstein wrote Freud in 1933 to solicit his opinion on why mankind engaged in war, Freud's reply included this comment:

> [T]here are two factors of cohesion in a community: violent compulsion and ties of sentiment ('identifications,' in technical parlance) between the members of the group. If one of these factors become inoperative, the other may still suffice to hold the group together. Obviously such notions as these can only be significant when they are the expression of a deeply rooted sense of unity shared by all.[27]

While Freud discusses society as an entity it seems to be one which is additive in nature, i.e., made up of parts which in sum constitute a whole. This is a psychologistic approach, quite at variance with the generally accepted sociological conception, first clearly enunciated by Durkheim, that society sui generis, operates according to its own principles. And if individuals in sum (Freud's "society") are an entity set against the individual (see the quote on page 73), the aggregate must have a character quite distinct from the individuals comprising it. But this sociological implication seems to have escaped Freud.

Further on in this epistle Freud wrote:

> We assume that human instincts are of two kinds: those that conserve and unify, which we call 'erotic' (in the meaning Plato gives to <u>Eros</u> in his <u>Symposium</u>), or else "sexual' (explicitly extending the popular connotation of 'sex'); and, secondly, the instincts to destroy and kill, which we assimilate as the aggressive or destructive instincts. These are . . . the well-known opposities, Love and Hate, transformed into theoretical entities. . . . All that brings out the significant resemblances between men calls into play this feeling of community, identification, whereon is founded, in large measure, the whole edifice of human society.[28]

For Freud social cohesion and social control often were coterminous. Individual self-denial (repression) of instinctual pleasures made libidinal energies available for cultural tasks. Freedom and happiness, including human sexuality, were laid upon the altar of civilization. Nevertheless, this sacrificial offering to which men had condemned themselves did not nullify the irremediable antagonisms between instinctual demands and the restrictions of civilization. This irrevocable conflict constituted the main theme of <u>Civilization</u> <u>and</u> <u>its</u> <u>Discontents</u>.

Here Freud pursues his assumption concerning the inborn existence of antisocial tendencies which must be repressed, with society operating as the instrument of this repression. It is at least equally tenable to assume that human energies are directed toward socially approved ends because such conformity is rewarded. Thus a cognitive process is implicated in human development not merely a repressive one. In time the externally provided reward becomes internalized, i.e., the individual is pleased by his socially compliant behavior. Freud in fact dealt with the dynamics of this process which will be alluded to in the discussion of the family in the following chapter.

denies him the possibilities of happiness. Thus he failed to recognize that man, in interaction with others, creates and modifies both the conditions of his existence and the definition of what constitutes human happiness. He did see the external world as moderating individual behavior by influencing the transformation from pleasure principle to reality principle. However, to say that civilization, <u>as such</u>, denies human satisfactions generalizes human societies as necessarily repressive without regard to man as an active agent in the construction of that civilization. Even if Freud had been familiar with Mead's work on symbolic interactionism, and there is no evidence he was, it appears unlikely he would have taken seriously Mead's essentially cognitive approach to human relationships.

Freud had yet another idea concerning how men could attain a grasp of reality, which had the further merit of binding them to the human community.

> No other technique for the conduct of life attaches the individual so firmly to reality as . . . work; for his work at least gives him a secure place in a portion of reality, in the human community.[18]

Freud perceptively cited work's value for displacing self-aggrandizing, aggressive and erotic drives. This was as valuable as its material benefits. He could not refrain from adding that men were not made happy by their labors.

> The great majority . . . only work under . . . necessity, and this natural aversion . . . raises most difficult social problems.[19]

Freud's assessment of the significance of work appears in sharp contrast with that of Durkheim. Both recognized the importance of work for personal attachment and social solidarity. However, Durkheim stressed the web of interdependence thus created--an organic solidarity--which made work a preeminently <u>social</u> act; Freud's view of work as a means for displacement of inner drives of a potentially divisive charcter made work a <u>psychologically</u> motivated act whose social consequences were a secondary phenomenon.

with certain <u>innate givens</u>. Here the divergence of psychological and sociological perspectives appears quite clearly.

In another context Freud rooted the social in the individual by remarking that

> [Our] possibilities of happiness are . . . restricted by our constitution. . . . [The] attempt to procure . . . happiness and a protection against suffering through a delusional remolding of reality is made by a considerable number of people in common.[16]

Freud identified three sources of human suffering.

> We are threatened with suffering from three directions: from our body, which is doomed to decay and dissolution . . . ; from the external world, which may rage against us with overwhelming and merciless forces of destruction; and finally from our relations to other men. The suffering which comes from this source is perhaps more painful to us than any other. . . . Here too a piece of unconquerable nature may lie behind [the failure to achieve satisfying social relationships]--this time a piece of our own psychical constitution. . . .
>
> It is no wonder if, under the pressure of [such] suffering, men . . . moderate their claims to happiness--just as the pleasure principle itself, indeed under the influence of the external world, changed into the more modest reality principle. . . . [17]

Here Freud once again expressed his conviction that civilized society exacts a price in denial of human satisfactions, which themselves are rooted in individual constitutional needs.

When Freud spoke of people's "remodeling of reality" he seemed to open the door to the social construction of reality. But then he reverted to a familiar axiomatic position--man's innate constitution

Men's reluctant but necessary participation in some form of productive labor which made social existence possible was abetted by four institutionalized palliatives: <u>religion</u>, which compensated for feelings of isolation and weakness and promised later rewards for compliance; the <u>use of mind-altering substances</u> (alcohol, narcotics, etc.) which diminished the pangs caused by outrageous fortune; <u>art</u>, which offered

> subsitutive satisfactions for the oldest and still most deeply felt cultural renunciations and for that reason . . . serves as nothing else does to reconcile a man to the sacrifices he has made on behalf of civilization. On the other hand, the creation of art heightens his feelings of identification . . . by providing an occasion for sharing highly valued emotional experiences.[29]

And finally there were <u>science and technology</u>, which offset man's limited ability to comprehend and deal with nature. Nevertheless, social organization remained burdensome. There was no relief from the physical sufferings to which human organisms were vulnerable or to the repressions of civilization, however transformed into various cultural forms they might be. Ordinary unhappiness was ubiquitous, and individual neurosis a frequent consequence.

The most severe challenge to social stability, greater even than the sexual impulses, was man's inherent and ineradicable aggression. It

> reigned in primitive times . . . and it shows itself in the nursery . . . ; it forms the basis of every relation of affection and love among people (with the possible exception of the mother's relation to her male child).

> If we do away with personal rights over material wealth, there still remains prerogative in the field of sexual relationships. . . . If we were to remove this factor, too, by allowing complete freedom of sexual life . . . this indestructable feature of human nature will follow it there.[30]

In the same grim vein Freud asserted

> Homo homini lupus. Who, in the face of all his experience of life and of history, will . . . dispute this assertion? It . . . reveals man as a savage beast to whom consideration toward his own kind is something alien. . . .
>
> In consequence of this primary mutual hostility of human beings, civilized society is perpetually threatened with disintegration. The interest of work in common would not hold it together; instinctual passions are stronger than reasonable interests. Civilization has to use its utmost efforts to set limits to man's aggressive instincts and to hold [their] manifestations in check by psychical reaction- formations. Hence, therefore, the use of methods . . . to incite people into identifications and aim-inhibited relationships of love, hence the restriction upon sexual life, and hence too the ideal's commandment to love one's neighbor as oneself.[31]

Instinctual renunciations, work, and other cultural adaptations already cited (and some still to be discussed) were essential if civilization was to survive. Abolition of civilization would leave man in a state of nature in which indulgence in unbridled impulse gratification would destroy him. "It was precisely because of these dangers that we came together and created civilization."[32] Hobbes was no more explicit.

Freud believed he had discovered in his clinical work the presence of ineluctable aggression in man. This drive posed an ever-present threat to the maintenance of social organization. Nevertheless, there seems a hint of bafflement in Freud's attempts to deal with the concept. As will be seen Freud included a "must be" rationale for its existence. In both <u>Civilization and its Discontents</u> and <u>The Future of an Illusion</u> he discussed this troublesome hypothesis.

> [B]esides the instinct to preserve living substance and to join it into ever larger units, there must exist another, contrary instinct seeking to dissolve those units and to bring them back to their primaeval, inorganic state .... as well as Eros there was an instinct of death.... The instinct of destruction, moderated and tamed, and ... inhibited in its aim must, when it is directed toward objects, provide the ego with the satisfaction of its vital needs and with control over nature. ... [T]he assumption of the existence of the instinct is mainly based on theoretical grounds.[33]

Freud continued his assessment of the functional significance of the instinct of aggression:

> [T]he inclination to aggression is an original, self-subsisting, instinctual disposition in man, and ... it constitutes the greatest impediment to civilization.... [C]ivilization is a process in the service of Eros, whose purpose is to combine single human individuals, and after that families, then races, peoples and nations, into one great unity, the unity of mankind. ... These collections of men are to be libidinally bound to one another. Necessity alone, the advantages of work in common, will not hold them together. But man's natural aggressive instinct, the hostility of each against all and of all against each, opposes this programme of civilization. This aggressive instinct is the derivative and the main representative of the death instinct which we have found alongside of Eros and which shares world-dominion with it. ... [T]he struggle between Eros and Death, between the instinct of life and the instinct of destruction. ... is what all life essentially consists of ....[34]

What power could stem this torrential force? Freud advanced a thesis erected upon a familiar edifice: The individual-societal analogy. "This we can study in the history of the development of the individual."[35] Although Freud had cautioned he was speaking analogically rather than substantively when he referred to society in organismic terms, he used this device with sufficient frequency to suggest he thought of it in a literal sense. He wrote:

> Civilization . . . obtains mastery over the individual's dangerous desire for aggression by weakening and disarming it and by setting up an agency within him to watch over it, like a garrison in a conquered city.[36]

This is the superego which internalizes the aggression and directs it against the individual's own ego and in the form of conscience exhibits a sense of guilt, expressed as a need for punishment. The sense of guilt originates in early human helplessness with its attendant fear of loss of love and needed protection, or punishment. "At the beginning . . . what is bad is whatever causes one to be threatened with loss of love."[37]

The sense of guilt (which includes either deed or intention) derives from a dual source. Originally it arose from fear of an authority; later on it is generated by fear of the superego.

> First comes renunciation of instinct owing to fear of aggression by the <u>external</u> authority. (This is, of course, what fear of the loss of love amounts to, for love is a protection against this punitive aggression.) After that comes the erection of an internal authority, and renunciation of instinct owing to fear of it--owing to fear of conscience. In this second situation bad intentions are equated with bad actions, and hence comes a sense of guilt and a need for punishment. The aggressiveness of conscience keeps up the aggressiveness of the authority.[38]

Now Freud introduced the concept of the "cultural superego." Structurally, this superego represents society's ideals, transmitted through society's extra-familial agencies of socialization. In Freud's view, this superego owed its derivation to the charismatic influences of a civilization's great men.

> The analogy between the process of civilization and the path of individual development may be extended in an important respect. . . . [T]he community, too, evolves a superego under whose influence cultural development proceeds. . . . The superego of an epoch of civilization has an origin similar to that of an individual. . . . based on the impression left behind by the personalities of great leaders--men of overwhelming force of mind or men in whom one of the human impulses has found its strongest and purest, and therefore often its most one-sided, expression. In many instances the analogy goes still further, in that during their lifetime these figures were--often--mocked and maltreated. . . . In the same way, indeed, the primal father did not attain divinity until long after he had met his death by violence. The most arresting example . . . is . . . Jesus Christ. . . . Another point of agreement between the cultural and the individual superego is that the former, just like the latter, sets up strict ideal demands, disobedience to which is visited with 'fear of conscience.' . [39]

Freud not only reaffirmed the individual-society analogy but also echoed such contemporaneous German philosophers as Nietzsche and Spengler in their belief that the historical process essentially reflected the biographies of great men. Freud's interest in historically important personages was a significant component of his social thought which will be addressed later in this chapter.

The cultural superego was of immense importance to the stability of the social order for its effectiveness was inversely correlated with the need to maintain civilization by force.

> [E]very civilization rests on a compulsion to work and a renunciation of instinct and therefore inevitably provokes opposition from those affected. . . . Alongside of wealth we now came upon the means by which civilization can be defended--measures of coercion and other measures intended to reconcile men to it and . . . recompense them for their sacrifices. These latter may be described as the mental assets of civilization.
>
> . . . . It is in keeping with the course of human development that external coercion gradually becomes internalized; for a special mental agency, man's superego, takes it over and includes it among its commandments. . . . [T]he strengthening of the superego is a most precious cultural asset. . . . Those in whom it has taken place are turned from being opponents of civilization into being its vehicles. The greater their number is in a cultural unit the more secure is its culture and the more it can dispense with external measures of coercion.[40]

Men of a society are not influenced uniformly by the cultural superego. For some the innate aggressive drives become too much internalized thereby endangering their individual stability; for others, the aggressive drives were too little internalized, thereby posing a threat to social stability. Freud hoped that, with time, strengthening of man's intellect would lead to his more rational control of his physical world and governance of his instinctual drives. But would this gain in rationality be achieved in time to avert the ever-threatening outbreak of unleashed aggression? Freud's oft-quoted "The voice of the intellect is soft, but it does not rest till it has gained a hearing"[41] shines a ray of optimism from a generally bleak Freudian sky. In any event, some men, due to limited capacities, are utterly incapable of coping with the demands of civilization. These individuals become the outlaws, the isolates, the criminals, the psychotics of society except when exalted social position or charismatic qualities produce a great man or hero. Far beyond the capabilities of the recalcitrant masses were those men capable of sublimation.

> Sublimation of instinct is an especially conspicuous feature of cultural development; it is what makes it possible for higher psychical activities, scientific, artistic or ideological, to play such an important part in civilized life. [42]

In effect, the minority elite capable of creating high culture were essential to the continued existence of the social order.

> [C]ivilization . . . was imposed on a resisting majority by a minority which understood how to obtain possession of the means to power and coercion . . . It seems . . . every civilization must be built up on coercion and renunciation of instinct. [43]

Freud here elaborates his version of conflict theory, augmenting it with an elitist view of the leadership function.

> It is just as impossible to do without control of the mass by a minority as it is to dispense with coercion in the work of civilization. For masses are lazy and unintelligent; they have no love for instinctual renunciation. . . . It is only through the influence of individuals who can set an example and whom masses recognize as their leaders that they can be induced to perform the work and undergo the renunciations on which the existence of civilization depends. All is well if these leaders . . . possess superior insight into the necessities of life and [have mastered] their own instinctual wishes. But there is a danger that in order not to lose their influence they may give way to the mass more than it gives way to them, and it therefore seems necessary that they shall be independent of the mass by having means to power at their disposal. [44]

Freud is certain that the leaders must lead; vox populi is incapable of rendering sound judgments. In the following passage from Freud's previously cited Einstein letter, there is the unmistakable aura of Plato. Once again there is the invocation of the superior man, the philosopher-king.

> That men are divided into leaders and the led is but another manifestation of their inborn and irremediable inequality. The second class constitutes the vast majority; they need a high command to make decisions for them, to which decisions they usually bow without demur. In this context we would point out that men should be at greater pains than heretofore to form a superior class of independent thinkers, unamenable to intimidation and fervent in the quest of truth, whose function it would be to guide the masses dependent on their lead. . . . The ideal conditions would obviously be found in a community where every man subordinated his instinctive life to the dictates of reason.45

There is considerable irony in the fact that the cult of personality which characterizes the totalitarian state is the very type of society which was anathema to Freud because it denigrates the values which were so precious to him: the importance of the individual, freedom of thought and of inquiry, and tolerance of diversity.

The instinctual privations common to all mankind are differentially distributed. Envy exists toward those classes whose wealth or power exempt them from the degree of privation endured by the less favored classes. However, an identification process transforms resentment based on social stratification into social solidarity.

The narcissistic satisfaction provided by the cultural ideal is also among the forces which are successful in combatting the hostility to culture within the cultural unit. This satisfaction can be shared in not only by the favored classes, which enjoy the benefits of the culture, but also by the suppressed ones, since the right to despise the people outside it compensates them for the wrongs they suffer within their own unit. No doubt one is a wretched plebian, harassed by debts and military service; but, to make up for it, one is a Roman citizen, one has one's share in . . . ruling other nations. . . . This identification of the suppressed classes with the class who rules and exploits them is, however, only part of a larger whole. For on the other hand, the suppressed classes can be emotionally attached to their masters; in spite of the hostility to them they may see in them their ideals . . . .[46]

Freud's elitist ideas about leadership seem reminiscent of the thinking of Comte and Bagehot. It was necessary to "educate an upper stratum of men with independent minds."[47] There is also a flavor of Social Darwinism in Freud's warning that

Over and above the tasks of restricting the instincts . . . [there is] the danger . . . of a society . . . chiefly constituted by the identification of its members with one another, while individuals of the leader type do not acquire the importance that should fall to them in the formation of a group.[48]

Indeed, this constituted the substance of Freud's complaint about the United States. He saw America as a vulgar society characterized by the rule of popular sentiment instead of by those best qualified. Alexis de Tocqueville had a similar view of the tyranny of the majority. However, the Frenchman's visit to the U.S. induced some optimism about the potentials of popular rule which he acknowledged in his classic study, Democracy in America.[49]

Still other means existed to drain and displace peoples' aggression and thereby promote social cohesion. In Totem and Taboo Freud had argued that the very existence of social restrictions indicated the existence of impulses toward their violation. The state itself provided vicarious expression to man's aggressive impulses by its own aggressions.

> The state has forbidden to the individual the practice of wrong-doing, not because it desires to abolish it, but because it desires to monopolize it.[50]

And in Freud's epistle to Einstein he had written

> [W]e may define 'right' (i.e., law) as the might of a community. Yet it, too, is nothing else than violence, [against] whatever individual stands in its path.[51]

Group cohesion was enhanced, as well, by the availability of "outsiders" who could serve as scapegoats. Freud identified two readily available "wayward" entities:

> In this respect the Jewish people, scattered everywhere, have rendered most useful services. . . . One only wonders, with concern, what the Soviets will do after they have wiped out their bourgeois.[52]

Finally, man's aggression could be mobilized against an external enemy. Herein lay a root cause of war, one which also helped account for the intractable difficulties militating against its eradication. For if there were no object outside the group against which to unleash the inner furies of aggression, ceaseless civil war would threaten the social fabric.[53]

Before presenting and discussing Freud's views about social change some further comments will be made about his ideas concerning society.

To Freud social cohesion was problematic in view of the divisive effects of the sexual and aggressive drives he found innate in man. Hence mankind, for utilitarian reasons, achieved instinctual renunciations in preference to the anarchy of a "war of each against all." But Freud seems no more successful than earlier contract theorists in overcoming the circular reasoning implicit in such constructs. Contract theory assumes the prior existence of a commitment to play the game according to some established rules, thus assuming the prior existence of society.

Freud's social thought demonstrates a characteristic polarity: "The constitutional inclination of human beings to be aggressive towards one another"[54] was opposed by such cultural injunctions as the commandment to love one's neighbor as oneself. Freud saw human societies as systems of defense against inevitable individual anxiety. Man's insatiable drives, fated to be unrequited, were of such intensity they required social defenses for relief.

> [T]he history of civilization is no more than an account of the various methods adopted by mankind for 'binding' their unsatisfied wishes. . . .
> [T]he neuroses themselves have turned out to be attempts to find individual solutions for the problems of compensating for unsatisfied wishes, while the institutions seek to provide social solutions for these same problems.[55]

The idea that social insitutions functioned as adaptive processes for dealing with common psychological problems seems insightful. However, Freud apparently failed to reach beyond this problem-oriented reasoning to appreciate its additional, positive implications. Here his orientation to individual and social pathology may have narrowed his vision. The idea that individuals may discover and fulfill their potentials through their social relationships seems largely unrecognized in his thought. For him society meant the sacrifice of individuality. Freud thus overlooked the role of social institutions in promoting ego adaptations, creating identities, defining roles, etc. Freud viewed neurotic illnesses as

> asocial in their nature [and always aimed] at driving the individual out of society and at replacing the safe monastic seclusion of earlier days by the isolation of illness.[56]

This excerpt identifying Freud's view of neurosis as an isolating phenomenon offers further opportunity to critique his position. Once more Freud dichotomizes individual and society. There is the individual and there is society and certain mental processes (neuroses) point up the essentially separate nature of the two entities. The internal alienation reflected in neurosis accentuates the external alientation of the individual from his society. To be repetitive for the sake of emphasis: Freud's premise seems to be that individual and society are discrete. Certain influences promote their coalesence, others promote separateness. Freud seems inclined to conceptualize the individual prior to and apart from society; sociology sees this as contrary to its fundamental perspective of the individual self as a product (as well as fashioner) of the social process, and behavior as invariably responsive to, and intertwined with others.

Freud, lacking a sociological background, sometimes seemed more socially insightful in his clinical, empirically based work than in his social extrapolations. His conceptualization of the phenomenon of transference demonstrates his awareness of the fundamentally social nature of human functioning. Again and again Freud's patients behaved as though they carried in their heads representations of their past--parents, siblings, etc.-- which they imposed upon (transferred to) their current relationships. Freud repeatedly found himself regarded (unconsciously) as a father or lover or some other figure from his patient's past. As he discerned what was happening in his therapeutic relationships he both reshaped his analytic technique and used the transference as grist for the analytic mill. This certainly was not "safe monastic seclusion," the "isolation of illness." Freud was dealing with his patient's reconstruction of reality. Neurotic illness, then, is a social act. Freud perceived this clinically, yet he did not recognize it in a broader frame of reference.

To reflect further upon Freud's view of society as necessarily repressive: It is not really paradoxical to say that freedom may be nourished under conditions of social constraint. The force of law constrains, but it also may protect the individual in the exercise of his rights. Tradition may support repression, but it may also sanction expression of idiosyncratic behavior. Social institutions are also developed through cognitive processes, are not merely constructions reactive to psychic drives. Freud's deterministic bent kept him from sharing George Herbert Mead's insight that human behavior has an emergent quality, is never completely determined by the influence of antecedent events. It is too bad the two thinkers never met!

Freud spoke in the unmistakable accents of conflict theory, but oblivious to Marx's socially based conflict theory and without the advantages of the contemporary labeling perspective. His metaphor for the superego was a "garrison occupying a conquered city." As he saw it, inside every civilized man, a wild man struggled to escape. The individual in conflict was extrapolated to the social order, for conflict existed on both these levels. The social entity was the analog of the individual entity.

Karl Marx also was interested in the coherence of the two levels. For him, too, linkage between the social order and the destiny of the individual had been established. But where Marx saw social organization as the independent variable, Freud's paradigm explained social phenomena in terms of the characteristics of individual human nature. Freud acknowledged that changes in property relations would mitigate human aggression much more than ethical precepts, but only the socialists, he felt, could be naive enought to believe such changes would suffice. As he brought Civilization and its Discontents to a close Freud wrote

> there is one question which I can hardly evade. If the development of civilization has such a far-reaching similarity to the development of the individual and if it employs the same methods, may we not be justified in reaching the diagnosis that, under the influence of cultural urges, some civilizations, or some epochs of civilization-- possibly the whole of mankind--have become 'neurotic?' . . . But we should . . . not forget . . . we are only dealing with analogies. . . . Moreover, the diagnosis of communal neuroses is faced with a special difficulty. In an individual

neurosis we take as our starting-point the contrast that distinguishes the patient from his environment, which is assumed to be 'normal.' For a group all of whose members are affected by one and the same disorder no such background could exist; it would have to be found elsewhere. . . . But in spite of all these difficulties, we may expect that one day someone will venture to embark upon a pathology of cultural communities.⁵⁷

Since Freud's time several barks have ventured but none seems to have reached a friendly port.⁵⁸

Freud once again raises questions of social constructionism, ideology and the relativity of culture without, however, identifying them as such or exploiting their implications. The definition of social reality is not, as Freud surmised, an objective given, but is man-made. There is no Archimedean vantage point, outside the world, on which to stand in order to assess objective social reality. Social reality thus becomes what people within a society define it to be. The U. S. defines the nature of the Soviet state as inimical to American interests; the Soviet union defines the U.S. as hostile to its own security. Sub-cultural groups illustrate the same principle. The psychiatric profession defines mental illness from its own behavioral frame of reference: deviance from predetermined behavioral norms signifies illness. Thomas Szasz, a maverick psychoanalyst, believes such attribution rests upon a more mythical than factual foundation.⁵⁹ This is because it does not consider varying cultural definitions of appropriate and inappropriate behavior. Conventional psychiatric definitions also are heedless of the impact of labeling in defining who is mentally ill.

Social Change

Freud saw mankind involved in a process of cultural development and change which had been underway from time immemorial. Much had been accomplished of a "positive" nature: a progressive erosion of instinctual control of behavior, a strengthening of the intellect which helped master instincts, and an introversion of the aggressive impulse. On the other hand, the turning inward of aggression constituted a peril of undetermined consequences, and cultural development had impaired the sexual function in civilized man. The energies devoted to sexual impulses had been displaced to cultural pursuits. In consequence, the more cultural "races" and the more cultured elements of society were experiencing a growing population disparity in favor of the "uncivilized" and "backward" peoples.

Freud had developed his social thought from a foundation of clinical observations of individual psychopathology. In dealing with social change Freud integrated his clinical observations with prevailing ideas concerning social evolution. Freud employed an anlogy akin to that used by Comte and Spencer, namely, that the individual mind in its development recapitulates stages of human history. He relied upon the anthropological literature of his time, especially the psychology of "primitive" peoples. These works, especially Frazer's Golden Bough, employed the analogy of primitive and child. Here the hypothesized primitive era of civilization constituted the childhood of the human race. Freud inverted the image, to make childhood the primitive phase in the life history of the individual. During the childhood years, asserted Freud, the immense evolutionary gap between stone age man and his civilized descendant was traversed. In support of this assertion Freud averred that primitive peoples experienced the very feelings and emotions that were apparent in contemporary primitives, i.e., children.

In both Totem and Taboo and Moses and Monotheism Freud described an evolution of mind which reproduced the Comtean triad of social stages. This correlation between historical stages of society and libidinal development of the individual went as follows: The individual's libido undergoes progressively widening scope from investment in oneself (Stage One), to investment in one's parents (Stage Two), and ultimately to other adults (Stage Three). Analogically, man's view of the world has evolved from animistic or mythological conceptions (Stage One) to the religious (Stage Two) and finally to the scientific (Stage Three).

At the animistic stage men ascribe omnipotence to themselves. At the religious stage they transfer it to the gods, but do not seriously abandon it themselves, for they reserve the power of influencing the gods in a variety of ways according to their wishes. The scientific view of the universe no longer affords any room for human omnipotence; men have acknowledged their smallness and submitted resignedly to death and the other necessities of nature.[60]

Representations of these parallel stages appears in Figure 1 on the following page. An additional observation which Freud wrote during the first world war presents another facet of his social evolutionary thought. He wrote:

> [T]he evolution of the mind shows a peculiarity which is present in no other process of development. When a village grows into a town, a child into a man, the village and the child become submerged in the town and the man . . . . The old materials or forms have been superseded and replaced by new ones. It is otherwise with the development of the mind. . . . in this case every earlier stage of development persists alongside the later stage which has developed from it; the successive stages condition a co-existence. . . .
> Perhaps [nations] are reproducing the course of individual evolution, and still today represent very primitive phases in the organizational formation of higher unities.[61]

Man's distinguishing characteristic, his capacity for culture, established the inevitability of repression and inner conflict, a heightened sense of guilt and therefore a proneness to neurosis. Man was both the rational animal and the repressed animal. Repression and socialization represented inner and outer aspects of the same functional process.

Nineteenth century thought was rife with conflict theory, so it is not surprising that conflict occupied a central place in Freud's thought. Darwinian theory concerning intra-species conflict applied to social theory meant institutionalizing a competitive struggle

FIGURE 1
SEQUENCE OF DEVELOPMENTAL STAGES IN INDIVIDUAL AND SOCIETY

Stages of Individual Development	Radius of Social Relationships (Object Choices)	Reality Orientation (Man's View of Causation)	Stages of Societal Development
Infancy → → → →	Narcissism (Focus on Self) →	Spirits (including those group members now dead) → → → →	Animism
Childhood → → → → → → →	Parents (Family) → → → → → →	Gods → → → → → → → → → (whom men may influence)	Religion
Adulthood → → → → → → → →	Mature Heterosexual → → → Object Choice	Positivistic (Abandonment of omnipotence of thought – except in the unconscious; renunciation of pleasure principle for reality principle) → → → →	Science

for existence; conflict was a necessary instrument of "progress." This lent credibility to Freud's conceptions of intra-human and individual-society conflict. The same could be said of Adam Smith's "unseen hand" guiding economic progress through the operation of freely competing market forces. Also there was Marx's thesis and antithesis of class conflict as the explantory dynamic for society's political transformations. To these Freud added id and superego antagonisms and the struggle of the immortal antagonists <u>Eros</u>, the forces of life and love, and <u>Thanatos</u>, the forces of death, destruction and dissolution. Culture provided both the impetus and the means to sublimate libido into socially constructive activities (art, science, etc.), and aggression into technological subjugation of nature. These activities built culture.

Freud believed in a fundamental conflict between individual and society. A coercive society is mandated by the inability of the masses of men to overcome their slothful and impulse-ridden ways. Given that "men are not spontaneously fond of work" and that "arguments are of no avail against their passions" these "two widespread human characteristics"[62] necessitated powerful leaders and a coercive society. Society, then, must be stratified, comprised of unequals, bonded by fundamentally irrational ties to leaders who are symbolic representatives of the father. In this sense the state represented an extension of the family.

To describe men as fundamentally slothful and impulse-ridden is to leave out the influence of the social structure and its corresponding ideological formulas for the conduct of life. Would Freud say that the Greek and Buddhist ideal of the contemplative life, unburdened by acquisitiveness, indicated a fundamental slothfulness among adherents? Freud firmly believed in the work ethic which, as Max Weber[63] pointed out, contributed to the rise of capitalism. There was a "goodness of fit" between acquisitive, thrifty, contained and future-oriented men and the accumulation of captital for business enterprise. Under such circumstances to be slothful was to be socially deviant, condemned as immoral or weak. But a recent generation-long interval of high technology and the resultant diffusion of affluence even to the skilled blue-collar level elevated the pursuit of leisure to a value shared by rich and non-rich alike. Did man's innate nature suddenly change? Hardly, and does this not demolish any theory of innate attitudes toward work, slothful and otherwise? Historical change seems more reasonably a function of altered social conditions than of the action of exceptional human beings. This point is further discussed below.

In discussing Freud's analogizing of family and state Rieff avers that, perhaps unwittingly, Freud subverted political authority and social control. Freud had said:

> From the time of puberty onward the human individual must devote himself to the great task of <u>freeing himself from the parents</u>. . . . These tasks are laid down for every man; it is noteworthy how seldom . . . they are solved in a manner psychologically as well as socially satisfactory.[64]

Rieff makes the perceptive observation that if outgrowing parental authority is necessary to individual health, yet filial piety is necessary to social stability, then social rebellion assumes normative significance.[65]

Freud did recognize that there are socially disruptive pressures based upon inequalities and inequities in the distribution of power.

> Social life is always complicated by the fact that, from the onset, the group includes elements of unequal power, men and women, elders and children, and very soon, as a result of war and conquest, victors and the vanquished--i.e., masters and slaves--as well. From this time on the common law takes notice of these inequalities of power, laws are made by and for the rulers, giving the servile classes fewer rights. Thenceforward there exist within the state two factors making for legal instability, but legislative evolution, too: first, the attempts by members of the ruling class to set themselves above the law's restrictions and, secondly, the constant struggle of the ruled to

extend their rights and [secure] . . .
equal laws for all . . . laws may
gradually be adjusted to the changed
conditions or . . . insurrections and
civil wars [are] followed by a new
regime of law. There is another factor
of [pacific] constitutional change
. . . cultural evolution of the
mass[es] . . . .[66]

When considering social change the figure of Marx inevitably reappears as a foil to psychoanalytic thought. For Marx the constant underlying historical change was contending economic interests. For Freud the constant was human nature. Change occurred as the species developed. Freud's approach was essentially ahistorical. Internal conflict, the strife between the individual and his repressive civilization, and the ineradicable influence of the past suggested the immutability of history. On the other hand, by analogizing society to the individual, who does develop and change, Freud presumed an evolutionary thrust in society. On the one hand, by the method of analogy, time leads to unilinear progress, the ultimate primacy of the soft but persistent voice of the intellect; on the other, via the conception of the prototype, time never changes. Masculine and feminine nature, the ageless and repetitive oedipal struggle in each generation, mean a fatalistic closed circle of change. Even the most dramatic form of change, that of revolution, was a form of father-rebellion and doomed, like its prototype to fail. People had best face the world as it is--and as it will be.

Clearly, Freud's view of society has conservative implications. When the fundamental ambivalence felt by followers ("children") toward leaders ("fathers") precipitates social unrest, social change consists of transfer of the father persona. The prototype of the follower's esteem of the ruler is found in "the relation of the child to its father"[67] projected on a societal scale. The fundamental ambivalence toward rulers rests not upon a considered judgment of their short-comings but on unconscious hostile feelings, for all relationships are fundamentally ambivalent. As the ruled ascribe illusory powers to their leaders so also do they retain hostile feelings toward them.

This analogue between parents and rulers implies that social action is a projection of personal emotions, social protest a neurotic symptom, thereby justifying and supporting an authoritarian ideology. <u>Moses and Monotheism</u> espouses the Freudian view of political leadership. He appeared to be intrigued by

> how impossible it is to dispute the personal influence upon world-history of individual great men, what sacrilege one commits against the splendid diversity of human life if one recognizes only those motives which arise from material needs . . . .[68]

Political leaders represented, to Freud, a collective projection of the cultural superego. Presumably when these elites fail as exemplars and protectors they lose their legitimacy and social conflict is exacerbated.

Marx saw political adherence as a response to one's class position. Freud saw this as an outgrowth of attachment to a political "father." The latter

> puts the stamp of his moral character on his followers, as Moses (Freud's favorite example) created the Jewish character . . . . There can be no differences over principles but only among competing personal identifications.[69]

Does this suggest that dissidence and revolution express neurotically displaced aggression against the father? So it would seem, for the social is defined in psychological terms. Social phenomena are manifest content; they make psychological mechanisms explicit within a social context.

Systems which purport to explain man's fate at some point appear to lock men into a fateful changelessness. Economic determinism, biological, and even cultural determinism share this characteristic. Marx resolved his dilemma of how men could effect change in a deterministic system. Men at some time could be masters of their fate because they could become aware of their class interests. Thereby they would transform themselves into agents rather than objects of social change. Freud's solution was to maintain an abiding faith in the ultimate triumph of

the reason. Where id was, there ego shall be. The
soft voice of the intellect did not rest until it
gained a hearing. Finally it would succeed.

> This is one of the few points on which
> one may be optimistic about the future
> of mankind, but it is in itself a point
> of no small importance. And from it one
> can derive yet other hopes. The primacy
> of the intellect lies, it is true, in a
> distant, distant future, but probably
> not in an <u>infinitely</u> distant one.[70]

In the short run (which he did not define) Freud
was less sanguine; nevertheless, the door to change
was left ajar--in this instance by the weight of
civilization itself, a burden so oppressive that in
time men might refuse to bear it any longer.

Early on, Freud had written

> Experience teaches us that for most
> people there is a limit beyond which
> their constitution cannot comply with
> the demands of civilization.[71]

Later he asserted that

> every individual is virtually an enemy
> of civilization . . . . [L]ittle as men
> are able to exist in isolation, they
> . . . nevertheless feel as a heavy
> burden the sacrifices which civilization
> expects of them in order to make a
> communal life possible. Thus
> civilization has to be defended against
> the individual. . . . [72]

It was true, in Freud's view, that repression was
carried out in the interests of the reality principle,
in order to safeguard the pleasure principle. Thus in
theory social demands and individuality were
normatively consistent. However, empirically they
came into conflict.

Freud's pessimism is a byword among his critics.
Nevertheless, his letter to Einstein, to which
references have already been made, "prescribed" a
course for mankind which seems achievable, and which
indicates he felt mankind might yet prosper in a
social psychological sense.

But, for the transition from crude violence to the reign of law, a certain psychological condition must first obtain. The union of the majority must be stable and enduring. If its sole raison d'etre be the discomfiture of some overweening individual and, after his downful, it be dissolved, it leads to nothing. Some other man . . . will seek to reinstate . . . violence and the cycle will repeat itself. . . . Thus the union of the people must be permanent and well organized; it must enact rules to meet the risk of possible revolts; must set up machinery ensuring that such acts of violence as the law demands are carried out. This recognition of a community of interests engenders among the members of the group a sentiment of unity and fraternal solidarity which consitutes its real strength . . . .

There is but one sure way of ending war and that is the establishment, by common consent, of a central control which shall have the last word in every conflict of interests. For this, two things are needed: first, the creation of such a supreme court of judicature; secondly, its investment with adequate executive force.[73]

Further discussion of Freud's thought on the subjects of this chapter will appear in Chapter VI. The following chapter will deal with Freud's thought concerning social groups and two of society's major institutions, religion and the family.

NOTES

[1] Freud's translators rendered his term Kultur as both "Civilization" and "Culture" and the more sociologically relevant term "society" would also be consistent with Freud's meaning.

[2] Sigmund Freud, Civilization and its Discontents, Standard Edition, Vol. XXI, p. 95.

[3] Sigmund Freud, Totem and Taboo, Standard Edition, Vol. XIII, pp. 125, 126.

[4] Sigmund Freud, Moses and Monotheism, trans. by Katherine Jones, (New York: Random House, 1939), p. 104.

[5] J.A.C. Brown, Freud and the Post-Freudians (Baltimore: Penguin Books, 1964, p. 117.

[6] Sigmund Freud, Totem and Taboo, op. cit., p. 2.

[7] Sigmund Freud, Group Psychology and the Analysis of the Ego, Standard Edition, Vol. XVIII, p. 92.

[8] Alasdair MacIntyre, Herbert Marcuse, (New York: Viking Press 1970), p. 55, quoted from Marcuse, Eros and Civilization, 1954, p. 15.

[9] Sigmund Freud, Totem and Taboo, op. cit., p. 66.

[10] Ibid., p. 158.

[11] Ibid., p. 97.

[12] Sigmund Freud, The Future of an Illusion, Standard Edition, Vol. XXI, p. 3, quoted from 1935 postscript to Freud's An Autobiographical Study, 1935.

[13] Sigmund Freud, Three Essays on the Theory of Sexuality, Standard Edition, Vol. VII, p. 242.

[14] Sigmund Freud, Civilization and its Discontents, op. cit., p. 67.

[15] Sigmund Freud, Totem and Taboo, op. cit., p. 64.

[16] Sigmund Freud, Civilization and its Discontents, op. cit., pp. 76, 77, 81.

[17] Ibid., pp. 77, 86.

[18] Ibid., p. 80. (footnote)

[19] Ibid.

[20] Sigmund Freud, Totem and Taboo, op. cit., p. 144.

[21] Sigmund Freud, Civilization and its Discontents, op. cit., p. 117.

[22] Ibid., p. 94.

[23] Ibid., p. 95.

[24] Ibid.

[25] Ibid., p. 113.

[26] In psychoanalytic theory an aim-inhibited drive involves an erotic impulse whose aim of sexual union has been diverted without changing the erotic nature of the attachment.

[27] Sigmund Freud, "Why War?" In Civilization, War and Death, John Rickman, ed. (London: Hogarth Press, 1968), p. 89.

[28] Ibid., pp. 90, 94.

[29] Sigmund Freud, Future of an Illusion, op. cit., p. 14.

[30] Sigmund Freud, Civilization and its Discontents, op. cit., pp. 113, 114.

[31] Ibid., pp. 111, 112.

[32] Sigmund Freud, Future of an Illusion, op. cit., p. 15.

[33] Sigmund Freud, Civilization and its Discontents, op. cit., pp. 118, 119, 121.

[34] Ibid., p. 122.

[35] Ibid. p. 123.

[36] Ibid. pp. 123, 124.

[37] Ibid. p. 124.

[38] Ibid., p. 128.

[39] Ibid., pp. 141, 142.

[40] Sigmund Freud, Future of an Illusion, op. cit., pp. 10, 11.

[41] Ibid., p. 53.

[42] Sigmund Freud, Civilization and its Discontents, op. cit., p. 97.

[43] Sigmund Freud, Future of an Illusion, op. cit., pp. 6, 7.

[44] Ibid., pp. 7, 8.

[45] Sigmund Freud, "Why War?", op. cit., p. 84.

[46] Sigmund Freud, Future of an Illusion, op. cit., p. 13.

[47] Sigmund Freud, "Why War?", op. cit., p. 212.

[48] Sigmund Freud, Civilization and its Discontents, op. cit., p. 115, 116.

[49] Richard Hefner, ed., Alexis de Tocquiville, Democracy in America (New York: New American Library, 1961).

[50] Sigmund Freud, "Thoughts for the Times on War and Death," Standard Edition, IV, p.279.

[51] Sigmund Freud, "Why War?", op. cit., p. 85.

[52] Sigmund Freud, Civilization and its Discontents, op. cit., pp. 114, 115.

[53] Sigmund Freud, "Thoughts for the Times on War and Death," op. cit.

[54] Sigmund Freud, Civilization and its Discontents, op. cit., p. 142.

[55] Sigmund Freud, "The Claims of Psychoanalysis to Scientific Interest," Standard Edition, XIII, p. 186.

[56] Ibid., p. 188.

[57] Sigmund Freud, Civilization and its Discontents, op. cit., p. 144.

[58] A notable failure was a World War II work by an American psychiatrist "proving" Germany's "paranoid illness" caused her repeated international aggression. See Richard M. Brickner, M.D., Is Germany Incurable?, (Philadelphia: J. B. Lippincott, 1943).

[59] Thomas Szasz The Myth of Mental Illness (New York: Hoeber-Harper, 1961).

[60] Sigmund Freud, Totem and Taboo, op. cit., p.88.

[61] Sigmund Freud, "Thoughts for the Times on War and Death," 1915, Sander Katz, ed., in Freud: On War, Sex and Neuroses, trans. by Joan Riviere, et al. (New York: Arts and Science Press, New York, 1947), pp. 258, 259, 261.

[62] Sigmund Freud, The Future of An Illusion, op. cit., p.8.

[63] Max Weber, The Protestant Ethic and the Spirit of Capitalism, trans. by Talcott Parsons (New York: Scribners, 1930).

[64] Sigmund Freud, Introductory Lectures in Psychoanalysis, 1961-1971 (New York: Viking Press, 1959), p. 248.

[65] Philip Rieff, Freud: The Mind of the Moralist (New York: The Viking Press, 1959).

[66] Sigmund Freud, "Why War?", op. cit., p. 86.

[67] Sigmund Freud, Totem and Taboo, op. cit., p. 50.

[68] Sigmund Freud, Moses and Monotheism, Standard Edition, XXIII, p. 52.

[69] Rieff, op.cit., p. 244.

[70] Sigmund Freud, Future of an Illusion, op. cit., p. 53.

[71] Sigmund Freud, "Civilized Sexual Morality and Modern Nervous Illness," 1908, Standard Edition, IX, p. 191.

[72] Sigmund Freud, Future of an Illusion, op. cit., p. 6.

[73] Sigmund Freud, "Why War?", op. cit., pp. 85, 88.

CHAPTER V

SOCIAL GROUPS, THE FAMILY, AND RELIGION

Social Groups

The editor of Group Psychology and the Analysis of the Ego[1] noted that in this work Freud took up a train of thought derived from the final section of Totem and Taboo. These two works and Moses and Monotheism have provided most of the content for this chapter's initial section. Freud developed several more or less explicit propositions concerning social groups.

1. The psychology of groups is derived from the psychology of the individual mind.

2. "Group mind" begins its development in the libidinal relationships of family life.

3. Inherited mental characteristics provide predispositions which manifest themselves in the group mind.

4. Social groups, as microcosms of society, are hierarchically structured.

5. Groups are held together by libidinal ties toward the leader and identification between members stemming from their common tie to the leader.

6. Groups induce regressive behavior: a lessening of inhibitions and impaired cognition.

A summary of Freud's essential argument goes as follows: The intrinsic characteristic of a group, its binding force, is the aim-inhibited libidinal drives which exist between members. The latter share an identification with an ego-ideal, the leader and in consequence identify with one another. This constitutes a primary group, the critical components of which are shared emotional bonds based upon the dynamism of identification with a leader. The independent variable is the tie to the leader, for the attraction between members, hence the stability of the group, depends upon the stability of the leader-member tie. Disruption of the bond with the leader leads to group dissolution unless a new ego ideal supplants him.

The group exerts a powerful effect on members. Gratification of libidinal impulses reduces inhibitions, leading to more impulse-dominated behavior, and the group atmosphere also diminishes the ego's reality-testing function. A less autonomous individual emerges.

The archetypical primary group was the primal horde, which provides the model for group formation. The primal father now has been succeeded by the group leader but what earlier held true continues to be true: the direct expression of sexual impulses counteracts group formation and group unity.

Freud's social group theory stressed in two ways the centrality of the individual psyche. The individual was the source of those characteristics which initiated and promoted group interactions; a special individual, the leader, was largely responsible for a group's continued existence. Freud assumed as axiomatic that "individual" psychology was invariably social psychology because individual mental life always involved one or more "objects," i.e., other persons. Freud defined group psychology as

> concerned with the individual man as member of a race, of a nation, of a caste, of a profession, of an institution, or as a component part of a crowd of people who have been organized into a group at some particular time for some definite purpose.[2]

The mind is a collective entity, analogous in its functioning to the mentation characteristic in the individual.

> I have taken as the basis of my whole position the existence of a collective mind, in which mental processes occur

just as they do in the mind of an individual.³

Freud's idea of a "collective mind" invites comparison with Durkheim's conception of "collective representations." In the former case group solidarity rests upon commonly inherited and shared individual characteristics; the individual mind is analogized to the group mind. Durkheim's idea, however, referred to the collective experiences of a society over time. The group, as a whole, exceeds the limits of individual experience. The collective representations characterize a group and promote its unity. Such sentiments and ideas (the representations) elaborate the group's experiences over the generations, help members make sense of their experiences, and furnish them a world view. These representations encourage social solidarity, as does Freud's collective mind. But they are constructed from social traditions, hence are a manifestation of <u>social</u> heredity, not of Freud's biologically transmitted characteristics.

The quote above had appeared in <u>Totem and Taboo</u>, written in 1912. After a lapse of twenty-seven years Freud remained of the same persuasion.

> I hold that the concordance between the individual and the mass is . . . almost complete. The masses, too, retain an impression of the past in unconscious memory traces.⁴

Here Freud also affirmed--again--his conviction concerning inheritance of acquired characteristics. He regarded this hypothesis as indispensable to the psychic continuity of the generations. In the same work in which the above quotation appears (<u>Moses and Monotheism</u>) Freud acknowledged that his view, that acquired characteristics were transmitted, was disputed by biologists. Nevertheless, he had said in <u>Group Psychology and the Analysis of the Ego</u>, that

> Our conscious acts are the outcome of an unconscious substratum created in the mind mainly by hereditary influences. This substratum consists of the innumerable common characteristics handed down from generation to generation . . . .⁵

He repeated this at greater length in _Moses and Monotheism_. As he put it,

> there probably exists in the mental life of the individual not only what he has experienced himself, but also what he brought with him at birth, fragments of phylogenetic origin, an archaic heritage.[6]

Freud continued:

> [T]he archaic heritage of mankind includes not only dispostions, but also ideational contents, memory traces of the experiences of former generations . . . .
>
> . . . I have argued . . . there exists an inheritance of memory--traces of what our forefathers experienced . . . . When I speak of an old tradition still alive in a people, of the formation of a national character, it is such an inherited tradition . . . that I have in mind.
>
> . . . . If we accept the continued existence of such memory traces, then we have bridged the gap between individual and mass psychology. . .[7]

In these passages Freud offers two observations which merit comment. The first concerns his familiar argument concerning the hereditary transmission of acquired characteristics. The second is that individual minds are similarly constituted because of commonly held memory-traces; here Freud arrives at a kind of geometry of the mind: the whole (the "group mind") consists of the sum of its parts (individual minds).

As to the first point: no serious contemporary student of human biology supports the essentially Lamarckian position of inherited human memories. Certainly there are characteristic organically based and species-specific human predispositions, e.g., the capacity for speech, for erect posture, for toolmaking, etc.--but which language is spoken, under which circumstances an erect posture is appropriate, which tools "naturally" come to hand, are developments which require specific social circumstances for their realization. The immature human being requires a nurturing human environment, but he learns what it is to be human from experiences which build upon his human potential not, as far as we now know, upon inherited memories of human experiences.

As to the second point: the human propensity for "relatedness" does not require commonly held memory traces; rather, it is empirically evident that human associations fulfill universal human needs--for love, for cooperative problem-solving, for coming to terms with repetitively experienced socially based circumstances, such as family formation, care of the young, work, death, and other aspects of the human adventure. Freud really did not require any assumption of memory traces. Perhaps he felt the need for a bridging construct when he left familiar terrain of the individual psyche to venture into the relatively unfamiliar terrain of human groups.

As Freud's interests moved beyond the confines of clinical work, a broader conception of the nature of human interaction impelled him to reexamine love. His dark vision of human aggression and importunate sexuality underwent modification. Libido (energy of an unmeasured quantity) provided him the organizing principle for development of the group perspective. Libido represented a combining force which possessed many facets. A number of drives related to love. The nucleus of love was, indeed, sexual love with sexual union as its aim. However, love also included self-love, love of family members, friendship, generalized love of humanity, devotion to concrete objects and abstract ideas. All these, said Freud, emanate from the same instinctual impulses. Freud maintained there was nothing original in this wider use of the term, "love." Plato's Eros represents a love impulse of spacious dimensions, as does St. Paul's use of the word "charity" in his Epistle to the Corinthians. Love instincts are sexual instincts only in origin.

Love relationships, or emotional ties, constitute the essence of the group mind. The individual's willingness to yield his own distinctiveness and be amenable to suggestion (group influence) signifies the need, based upon love of others, to be in harmony rather than in opposition. The libidinal ties that bind group members extend both vertically and horizontally--above to the leader and laterally to the other members. The individual's relinquishing within the group of freedom of independent action is based upon those intense emotional ties. His self-love (narcissism) is limited because some libido has been redirected outward toward others. The character of these libidinal ties is aim-inhibited, i.e., "de-sexualized." In the group, love "instincts" are diverted from their original aims. Being in love involves withdrawal of ego from self--"encroachment upon the ego"[8] in Freud's phrase--and transfer to ties with the group.

> The same thing occurs in men's social relations as has become familiar to psychoanalytic research in the course of development of the individual libido. The libido attaches itself to the satisfaction of the great vital needs, and chooses as its first objects the people who have a share in that process. And in the development of mankind as a whole, just as in individuals, love alone acts as the civilizing factor in the sense that it brings change from egoism to altruism. And this is true both of sexual . . . and . . . desexualized . . . love.[9]

The group is a manifestation of a combining tendency. Freud cited Trotter's 1916 work, <u>Instincts of the Herd in Peace and War</u>, to buttress his belief in human gregariousness, the tendency to form ever larger social units, "The individual feels incomplete if he is alone."[10] At the same time this impulse toward grouping served to encourage conformity and made people more vulnerable to suggestibility. Although generally approving of Trotter's work Freud disagreed with the former's characterization of mankind as a herd animal. Freud claimed it would be more correct to identify man as a horde animal, i.e., an individual creature, in a horde led by a chief. Freud also went beyond Trotter in identifying love as a crucial component of the human animal's quest for unity. Love, by checking narcissism, became a factor in civilization.

A group, then, in its combining action demonstrated how the structures of social life arose out of a combination of "egoistic and erotic elements."[11] These socially oriented feelings sanctioned "showing consideration for another person without taking him as a sexual object."[12] Sexual impulses per se are antithetical to group solidarity because of their focus on exclusivity of the sexual union.

Superego formation, which is an outgrowth of the individual's resolution of the Oedipal situation, is a universal experience. Group membership supplants the individual superego with a collective ego-ideal, the leader. Thus "group mind" really begins its development in the family. Arlow comments:

What had previously been an intrapsychic relationship (the relation of the ego to its ideal) has now become an interpersonal relationship (the relation of the individual to the leader).[13]

Within the compass of the group a small-scale society is recreated which becomes a powerful agency for transformation of the individual. The person behaves differently than when he is in isolation. The individual superego, which had enabled the individual to monitor his behavior, is abandoned. Repressions may be dissolved, contagion and suggestibility may replace ordinary reality-testing as guides to behavior. The group becomes the authority to whom submission is owed. The individual experiences the "increased pleasure that is . . . obtained from the removal of inhibitions."[14] Intensification of affect undermines cognitive processes and group members become more vulnerable to loss of a sense of responsibility.

Freud here seems to be describing a crowd in terms of the "contagion" theory advanced in 1895 by LeBon. The process of contagion which influences group members seems a less mystical concept when examined in the light of contemporary sociological theory. It is true that members of crowds respond to the influence of others. Individuals become more suggestible, experience an enhanced sense of integration with others, and a blurring of the sense of personal identity. The focus of intellectual and emotional interest is narrowed, others are looked to for behavioral cues and individuals behave with less cognitive control.

111

However, the "contagion" theory suggests that crowd behavior is a uniquely different social phenomenon. It would be more parsimonious to accommodate crowd theory within an existing theoretical framework. This is what Ralph Turner has done with his "emergent norms" theory.[15] Turner argues that in the crowd new norms emerge in the process of social interaction. The behavior of those most active in the group sets the new rules of appropriate behavior for other members. Crowd behavior, therefore, is a special case of the general rule that prevailing social norms guide behavior. In crowds or other improvised groups the norms are created for the occasion, then enforced informally on group members.

Consistent with his overarching conception of an individual-family-group-societal progression Freud devoted attention in <u>Group Psychology</u> to the psychological development of the individual; he also had referred to intra-familial relationships, with specific reference to the Oedipus complex. He thus sought to marshall evidence for the prototypical nature of family and father in relation to groups and leaders. Group formations have their source in the circumstances of the primal horde and the leader epitomizes the primal father.

> [M]en have always known [instinctively] that once upon a time they had a primeval father and killed him.[16]

In the group the individual gives up his ego ideal and substitutes for it the group ideal as embodied in the leader, the "dreaded primal father." Why dreaded? Because every intimate emotional tie of a sustained nature contains ambivalence, the hostile component of which tends to be repressed from awareness. This profoundly important clinical discovery of Freud's (i.e., ambivalence) also finds a place in his social thought. The leader (father) is both venerated and resented. In the following, although Freud was speaking from a broad, societal frame of reference, he aptly represented his thinking about leaders of any scale.

> We know that the great majority of people have a strong need for authority which they can admire, to which they can submit, and which dominates and sometimes even ill-treats them.

We have learned from the psychology of the individual whence comes this need of the masses. It is the longing for the father that lives in each of us from his childhood days, for the same father whom the hero of legend boasts of having overcome . . . . all the features of which we furnish the great men are traits of the father [and] in this . . . lies the essence . . . of the great man. The decisiveness of thought, the strength of will, the forcefulness of his deeds, belong to the picture of the father; above all other things, however, the self-reliance and independence of the great man, his divine conviction of doing the right thing, which may pass into ruthlessness. He must be admired, he may be trusted, but one cannot help also being afraid of him. We should have taken a cue from the word itself; who else but the father should in childhood have been the great man?[17]

For Freud authority is personified. Social organizations concretize and exemplify authority in the person of the leader who is the recipient of the group's erotic feelings. A group presupposes a leader. When the libidinal ties dissolve a crisis ensues until a new leader can reconstitute and refocus the group's libidinal ties.

Max Weber saw the charismatic leader (a father figure in Freud's typology), inevitably giving way to the dominance of an impersonal bureaucratic apparatus. The implication of Freud's thought suggests that the bureaucratic organization, insofar as it succeeds instrumentally, incarnates the father. For Freud the (exalted) individual still counted. Freud was aware that coercive elements also were of significance in holding together certain formal organizations. However, Freud doubted that external force, relied upon to maintain integration and forestall structural alteration, would suffice. Efficient armies and institutionalized religions, said Freud, depend upon soldiers' and adherents' belief in the illusion that their leaders love them.

Freud here creates an ideology through the assertion of charismatic influences. The father reappears as the great man who creates social solidarity by drawing to him and focusing members' ties of sentiment. Whether, as Freud asserted, these ties are erotic in nature, remains problematic.

For Freud the leader's place in group structure was critical for comprehending group psychology. Leadership made it possible for group members to regress in obedience to this higher authority, to suspend individual conscience and to accept group norms which could support delinquent, uninhibited conduct not tolerated by the individual superego. Roazen has pointed out that existence of two moralities, public (group) norms and private (individual) norms had been anticipated by Machiavelli.[18]

But why should the person of the leader exert such profound influence, inducing submission? Love, the positive side of the ambivalent feeling was the key to obedience.

> [W]e will [advance] the suppostion that love relationships (or, to use a more neutral expression, emotional ties) . . . constitute the essence of the group mind.[19]

Social cohesion is a product of aim-inhibited libidinal ties. Affection for others overcomes self-love; in quest of the leader's approval group members embrace obedience. Sharing and mutual help, "the community of . . . egos"[20] is an outgrowth of accepting the leader as the ideal, of the members' identification with him and thus with each other. A group is defined by Freud virtually in those terms:

> . . . a number of individuals who have put one and the same object [the leader] in the place of their ego-ideal and have completely identified themselves with one another in their ego.[21]

Identification[22] was the operative concept in Freud's definition and explication of a group. He developed it originally in explanation of how the child experienced and mastered the intricacies of his oedipal involvement. Identification is the earliest emotional linking with another person, a molding of the ego after one taken as a model. It includes perception of a shared quality with someone who is himself not the object of the sexual instinct. It enables one person to empathize with another, thereby constraining aggression toward the other. Narcissism is partially replaced by helpfulness. Groups, Freud noted, tend to close ranks against non-members. From this observation Freud adduced an additional explanation of intergroup prejudice: the feeling of group cohesiveness was enhanced when animosity was mobilized against an "outside," numerically weaker minority. Anti-Semitism provided an example of this general principle.

Concluding Critique

A review of this area of Freud's thought reveals again his penchant for deriving the social from the individual. He maintains his adherence, via the logic of his embattled Lamarckian position, to the view that hypothesized events of a remote past persist in human memory. Even in Freud's day, as he acknowledged, this position was hardly tenable.

Freud's view of a hierarchically organized society which mirrored a family structure dominated by a patriarch seems more accurate as a reflection of the European society of his time. The same may be said of the extrapolation of his own Jewish middle-class family culture with its venerated and feared father. That such a society and such a family type existed seems beyond dispute. Its universality is another matter, as is that of the Oedipus complex. The issue is important because the latter's resolution was postulated to culminate in the father identification which formed the essential libidinal tie in groups. The generalization concerning group libidinal ties, therefore, is questionable at best.

Freud's view of the group as an extension of the family understandably lacks a contemporary, more sophisticated awareness. A more current view sees leadership not as an aspect of father identification but as a function of the group's tasks. Rather than the static conception reflected in Freud's view, a later appraisal sees leadership subject to alteration as the task alters. Where Freud saw the leader as the object of the group's ambivalent feelings and the repository of its superego, thereby facilitating sibling-like relations among members, the leader now is seen in instrumental terms, i.e., the criterion of task accomplishment is most relevant. Relationships among members and between them and the leader reflect real-life behaviors, relative maturity of members and success or failure in attaining group goals.

The essence of this criticism is that the instrumental function of groups was largely ignored by Freud. Though he referred to the Catholic Church and the army as examples, his essay on <u>Group Psychology</u> was essentially devoid of what groups do. Freud discussed intra-group currents of emotion which emanate from psychological needs while ignoring group activities which further socially defined goals.

This criticism would be one-sided, however, if it failed to recognize that Freud's attention to psychic processes also enriches social group theory. Max Weber had contributed to the methodology of the social sciences the idea that social phenomena were fundamentally explainable in terms of the actions of individuals. Freud added a significant additional dimension. Recognition of psychic processes within groups means that within the group entity the playing out of sibling rivalries and power motives, disjunction between public acts and private motives become legitimate objects of study and help explain groups' successes and failures. Group integration is a much more complicated achievement than assessment of conscious elements would suggest. The psychological aspects of groups, by now generally accepted, were hardly given serious attention before Freud.

The Family

The family, said Freud, is "the germ-cell of civilization."[23] This statement seems to accommodate several meanings. Freud regarded the family as the paradigm of all social aggregates, including the largest of all groupings, society itself. In another meaning, the statement attributes to the family the social structure within which individuals are socialized to the repressions necessary to social order, and to the attitudes and values necessary to social consensus. In yet another meaning family relationships are viewed as the source and the social matrix within which the Oedipus complex arises and is resolved. Through resolution of the Oedipus complex successive generations of sex-typed leaders assume their vital social roles, providing direction for society. For the individual the family is the first society and society is an extension of the family. Thus in Moses and Monotheism Freud noted

> In the . . . development of the . . . individual [the social order is reconstituted and] . . . the parents' authority--essentially that of the all-powerful father . . . wields the power of punishment--that demands instinctual renunciation on the part of the child and determines what is allowed and what is forbidden. What the child calls 'good' or 'naughty' becomes later, when society and superego take the place of the parents, 'good' in the sense of moral, or 'evil,' virtuous or vicious. But it is still the same thing: instinctual renunciation through the presence of the authority which replaced and continued that of the father.[24]

Thus, according to Freud, power disparities within the family facilitate socialization. The child is compelled to conform by superior force. However, the situation is more complex than that. The social order ultimately made possible by the child's instinctual renunciation is also generated by

> family feeling, with its erotic roots, which has induced . . . individuals to make this [instinctual] renunciation.[25]

Hence two separate though related forces, both compulsion and love, are at work within the family. The nature of their relationship will be dealt with in the exposition of this section. Compulsion originates as an external force. Parents (Freud would stress the father's role) impose upon the child the claims of the cultural environment. To make palatable the child's shift from a pleasure-seeking, impulse-dominated, egoistic orientation to a socialized awareness of, and compliance with the expectations of the social system, i.e., an altruistic orientation, the parents proffer love. This interpersonal exchange--of love for compliance--facilitates the child's progression from the pleasure principle to the reality principle. The process begins with the infant's awareness of parental responses of approval or disapproval of various behaviors. It shapes its behavior accordingly because its developing ego perceives the need for parental approval in order to have its needs met.

Thus far the process involves a quid pro quo, a performance exchange, as it were. However, the process becomes internalized, and here Freud postulated that this incorporation is abetted by acquired innate dispositions.

> We learn to value being loved as an advantage for which we are willing to sacrifice . . . . The external factor is the force exercised by upbringing . . . . Throughout the life of the individual there is a constant replacement of the external compulsion by the internal. The influences of civilization cause an ever-increasing transmutation of egoistic trends into altruistic and social ones, and this by an admixture of erotic elements. . . . [E]very internal compulsion . . . in the development of human beings was originally . . . in the evolution of the human race . . . an external one. Those . . . born today bring with them as an inherited consitution some . . . tendency (disposition) towards transmutation of egoistic into social instincts . . . .
> If we give the name of cultural adaptability to a man's personal capacity for transformation of the egoistic impulses under the influence of the erotic, . . . this adaptability [consists] of two parts, one innate and the other acquired through experience . . . . [26]

The process of internalization of the norms begins in early child-parent reciprocity with its obedience-love interchange. This leads inevitably to the elaboration of erotic relationships within the family. These reach their climax in the Oedipus complex. A great instinctual renunciation resolves the complex. The quest for gratification of erotic drives directed toward the parent of the opposite sex is abandoned. In place of the ambivalence felt toward the parent/rival, identification with this parent takes place. Identification provides the greatest impetus to formation of the superego for it entails the taking on of the parental "conscience." Thereby society, via the parent as agent, positions its normative structure "inside" the child. The latter becomes a bearer of the culture. This acquisition of civilized conscience depends upon love and the family

> and the fatal inevitableness of guilt . . . . for guilt is the expression of the conflict of ambivalence . . . . engendered . . . in the Oedipus complex . . . . that which began in relation to the father ends in relation to the community.[27]

Man's need of a family makes inevitable the progression described above. The internalized sense of guilt provides the great socializing force which both inhibits socially destructive behavior and places mankind under an oppressive psychic burden. It originates then in the fear of an authority (phylogenetically the primal father) and acquires a later source in the reproaches of the superego, the incorporated parental/social authority.

There is yet another dimension to the family's contribution to the socialization process. People conform to the norms as a matter of conscience; to do otherwise would exacerbate the sense of guilt. But, as Freud recognized, obedience to society's rules may turn out to be a matter of expedience.

> [Our] conscience is not the inflexible judge that ethical teachers are wont to declare it, but in its origin is dread of the community and nothing else.

> Education and environment offer benefits . . . of love, but also employ another kind of premium system, namely reward and punishment. In this way their effect may turn out to be that [the person] . . . will 'behave well' . . . although no involvement of instinct, no transformation of egoistic into altruistic inclinations has taken place . . . . [O]ne . . . acts rightly because his instinctual inclination

compels him . . . and the other is 'good' only insofar and for so long as such civilized behavior is advantageous for his own egoistic purposes.

Civilized society, which exacts good conduct and does not trouble itself about the impulses underlying it, has thus won over to obedience a great many people who are not thereby following the dictates of their own nature.[28]

This utilitarian (as opposed to libidinal) view of social conformity does not require much stretching to evoke Erving Goffman's dramaturgical model of social behavior. If the comparison is valid, Freud anticipates Goffman's version of a social self which employs "impression management"[29] as a technique for dealing with others.

Erik Erikson[30] has pointed out that "the first inequality in life is that of child and adult." Hence some adjustment to parental authority appears to be necessary in all societies. The family, then, is the prototype for authority and power relationships. Indeed, it is possible to alter Freud's conception and view the resolution of the Oedipus complex as the outcome of a power struggle in which the sexual element is of only secondary importance. Family relationships along the parent-child axis then become power relationships in which the larger and stronger segment of the axis must prevail. The outcome--the child's incorporation of parentally mediated societal norms--is the same, but the identification is with parental power, not with parental sexuality. The period of latency, which Freud hypothesized would follow the Oedipal resolution, might support this interpretation that power, not sexuality, is the root issue in the parent-child relationship.

Freud did, of course, assert that societies invariably are authoritarian. His paradigm established men's tasks to be the accommodation to authority; the corollary task of society was to legitimate the authority of suitably qualified men who would wield the power necessary for maintenance of the social fabric.

Having made his case for the family as requisite to the development of civilization, Freud again confronted his readers with a polarity. The family also poses a threat to civilized existence. The family, in addition to providing the setting for the socialization of each new generation, provides the most significant institutional arrangement for the legitimation and regulation of sexual expression. Because the family provides a socially sanctioned means of regulating genital (i.e., mature) sexual relationships, abolition of the family would, in Freud's view, lead to anarchy in sexual relationships. Eruption of uncontrollable conflict would follow. However, it is this human sexuality in itself which poses opposition to civilization. Freud believed sexuality was a stronger force in man than in any other species. In fact, it created the family.

In contrast with most other species man's sexual drive is constant. Moreover, the evolutionary changes which produced man's erect posture led, said Freud, to the primacy of visual stimuli over the olfactory and a continuity of sexual excitation which in turn led to the establishment of the primal family. This was because the male now had a motive for keeping the female at hand.

> The communal life of human beings had, therefore, a two-fold foundation: the compulsion to work which was created by external necessity, and the power of love, which made the man unwilling to be deprived of his sexual object--the woman--and made the woman unwilling to be deprived of the part of herself which had been separated off from her--her child. Eros and Anake (Love and Necessity) have become the parents of human civilization too.[31]

To the extent genital love promotes a mutual relationship of some intensity it is antithetical to civilization in that the unity of the two lessens the tie to the larger aggregate. These demands of social life exert a differential impact on men and women. Since the man possesses a finite quantity of libido, devotion to cultural aims (work; various creative tasks) requires the withdrawal of a corresponding amount of libidinal energy from women and from man's sexual life. Association with men also tends to alienate him from the husband and father role. In response to economic necessity sexual freedom must be curtailed. Freud again asserts his conflict perspective.

> In this respect civilization behaves toward sexuality as a people or stratum of its population does which has subjected another one to its exploitation.[32]

Freud presents a harsh picture of the antipathy between women in their family roles and civilization.

> [W]omen soon come into opposition to civilization and display their retarding and restraining influence, those very women who, in the beginning, laid the foundations of civilization by the claims of their love. Women represent the interests of the family and of sexual life . . . . [Civilization] has become increasingly the business of men . . . and compels . . . instinctual renunciation of which women are little capable . . . . a man must accomplish his tasks by . . . expedient distribution of his libido . . . . [T]he woman finds herself forced into the background by the claims of civilization and she adopts a hostile attitude toward it.[33]

A Critique of Freud's Views of the Family

Freud's personal preoccupation with the work ethic may well have made the conflict with sexuality described above seem self-evident. The stereotypical picture of the work-obsessed American middle-class male might lend some credence to this view. However, the overall contemporary situation appears to be at variance with this conception; at least the recent apparent proliferation, in contrast with Freud's time, of a more sensate outlook in the western world, makes his generalization at least questionable.

Freud's judgment of women seldom deviated from the sterotypical view presented above. A champion of individual rights, in opposition to the prevailing sexual hypocrisy,[34] he nevertheless remained faithful to the conventional view of women characteristic of his formative years and of the nineteenth century.

Another generalization, that families oppose the emancipation of their children, that they "will not give the individual up"[35] seems most valid as a generalization applicable to the patriarchal family system prevailing through the first two decades of the twentieth century. A struggle for autonomy was necessary to overcome the domination of the strong father. Nevertheless, despite the current ideology of emancipation which appears to promote generational autonomy, a continuing tension seems to exist in family life involving issues of family solidarity versus independence of the maturing offspring. Hence Freud's comment above retains contemporary relevance.

Freud's view of the origin of the human family stresses an essentially biologically rooted etiology: the satisfaction of the male sexual drive and the female nurturing impulse. The female's need of male protection during her caretaking role may be granted. However, there is less plausibility to the assertion of a biological basis for the male's maintenance of an ongoing bond. Could not the male satisfy mating needs without commitment to a permanent association? The male's greater size and strength afforded him physical dominance, enabling him to gratify his sexual desires without having to accede to any female demands for support and protection. The bisexual nature of human reproduction seems to provide a necessary but not sufficient cause for family life. Other, social factors would seem to be implicated in the institutionalization of the family in human society. Freud, in fact, recognized some of these, such as the regulating of sexual expression and the socialization of offspring. However, he apparently regarded these as derivative rather than primary.

By introducing the role of erotic drives in the socialization process Freud made a significant contribution to the perspective of social scientists. It was no more than common sense to recognize that family life civilized children. But wherein lay the impetus to the transformation from barbarian to functioning member of society? Freud's discussion of the role of love and the internalization of conscience added a dimension hitherto lacking. It was not merely the adult's power to compel obedience but the capacity of the child to <u>identify</u> with role models which was decisive. This conception detaches Freud from a purely biological perspective and places him among the social interactionists.

Once again Freud's dualistic thought is evidenced. The ubiquity of authority is a function of man's needs for restraint in his various social relationships--child and father, subject and ruler, citizen and society. One the other hand, Freud, ever the champion of the individual, asserted

> The liberation of an individual, as he grows up, from the authority of his parents, is one of the most necessary though one of the most painful results brought about by the course of his development . . . . Indeed, the whole progress of civilization rests upon the opposition between successive generations.[36]

Freud's generalizations about the family (indeed about all social institutions) assumed a universality and timelessness of institutional forms. Just as Hegel could not see beyond the Prussian state, Freud took the middle European late nineteenth and early twentieth century patriarchal family as the norm. Freud was a widely-educated person. Knowledge of literature, archaeology, philosophy, and other subjects enlarged his perspective and infused his writings. However, his clinical discoveries and later social constructs were based upon patient populations drawn largely from European industrial capitalist societies. This was a relatively homogeneous group with regard to culture and family type. Freud postulated a nuclear family and an intense mother-child bonding as necessary, "natural" and proper. Freud's ahistorical view is reflected in his failure to recognize the historical specificity of this family form. The Oedipus complex is a case in point. It assumes a strong patriarchal family dominated by a father who left child care in the hands of his wife. Thus Freud reified social arrangements and a sexual division of labor specific to a time and place.

Nancy Chodorow comments that ideologically

> women are located first in the sex-gender system, men first in the organization of production.
>
> Women in our society are primarily defined as wives and mothers, thus in

particularistic relation to someone else, whereas men are defined primarily in universalistic occupational terms.[37]

Two world wars brought women into the work place in enormous numbers and have accelerated mutations in sex roles. Subsequent macro-economic changes and increased urbanization in western societies have further redefined family functions. Ideological change again lags behind.

Freud certainly perceived accurately some family interactions which were occurring in his time and are valid now. Observations of pre-school children of contemporary American middle-class families provide anecdotal confirmation of behaviors which express transient "love triangles." Even so, there seems no way to establish the universality of the Oedipus complex or to test the association between repression of Oedipal drives and the development of conscience. Moreover, the role of "love" in parent-child relations differs from one culture to another. In contemporary western societies this love becomes eroticized to a degree quite unknown in some other societies. There parent-child bonds are maintained in an atmosphere of parental aloofness. This is so strikingly different from the familiar western pattern that outside observers have described it as "rejecting."[38]

There are other theoretical issues of considerable import. The functionalist account of morality and the Hobbesian generalizations about human nature underlie Freud's conclusions about morality, and these are by no means established facts. Any generalization about the social utility of all moral beliefs remains to be demonstrated. Perhaps all that can be said is that the Freudian version of morality possesses, in Jonathan Glover's phrase, "a certain intuitive plausibility."[39] Thus parental commands and prohibitions, common enough in childhood may, through the process of identification with the loved or feared parent, become the commands of later life. Their strength is derived from guilt following failure to obey the original source of one's gratifications and protection.

But plausibility is not synonymous with validity. Moreover, such a version of morality cannot encompass the subject unless morality is narrowly defined as consisting of arbitrary commands sanctioned by guilt feelings. This is a morality heavily deterministic and devoid of Freud's own definition of the ultimate human achievement: reason.

The contemporary western monogamous family, based upon an ideal of romantic love and affectional ties, emphasizes competition and possessiveness which reflect the ethos of capitalism. This encourages the rivalry and exclusive "possession" of the loved object which provides the seed bed out of which family romantic triangles emerge. From this base the identification and incorporative processes encourage the development of a "like father-like son" morality.

But ongoing experience and the ego's development of reason emancipate the person from the imperatives of early childhood. Indeed, there would be no escape from an endlessly repetitive and rigid normative structure if the mature individual remained a moral clone. However, Freud failed to credit the possibility of moral autonomy in the masses of men.

What then remains of Freud's contribution to understanding the supremely human function of value construction? His view of a primitive system of morality activated by guilt seems over-simplified and reductionistic. Nevertheless, Freud provided a plausible operational basis for the study of morality. The internalization of parental strictures which reflect societal norms, and their social function in channeling and controlling the intense affective currents of family life, represent Freud's contribution to the origins of morality. He cannot provide an all-encompassing explanation, but he contributes to our understanding of this complex subject.

Freud's primal horde concept is woven inextricably into his treatment of family origins and evolution. Therefore, the issue of the concept's validity is of considerable importance. Kenneth Burke provides an interesting perspective on the question of validity as it relates to the primal horde concept. In his essay, "The Temporizing of Essence" Burke points out the importance of translating "back and forth between logical and temporal vocabularies." Many concepts that might otherwise be discarded can thus be salvaged. Burke cites Otto Neurath's proposal, in <u>Foundations of the Social Sciences</u>, to abandon "cause-effect phraseology" in favor of a "growing-out-of phraseology."[40] This may be applied to Freud's use of the primal horde concept, borrowed, as he acknowledged, from Darwin. If one abandons a historicist conception of the idea, i.e., a belief in its historical existence and sees it as a statement about essence, anthropological data disproving the theory become irrelevant. The fact a primal horde cannot be demonstrated as a historical fact is not the point. If the primal horde is regarded as a description of the essence of certain societal relationships of Freud's time the concept has heuristic merit despite its existential discrediting. Indeed, Freud himself felt no need to advocate its literal truth, remarking,

> To be sure, this is only a hypothesis . . . to lighten the darkness of prehistorical times--a "Just-So-Story," . . . but I think it is creditable to such a hypothesis if it proves able to bring coherence and understanding into more and more new regions.[41]

Freud's analysis of the patriarchal family of his time convinced him of the reality of a family constellation characterized by rivalries and ambivalence. The literal existence of the primal horde was not the real issue; rather, it was the essence of family relations Freud sought to describe. In pursuit of his objective, that of analyzing the affective currents in the family life characterizing his own time and social setting, Freud was successful.

Religion

Freud's interest in religion was reflected in writings which spanned the final three decades of his life. This interest persisted from publication of a paper, "Obsessive Actions and Religious Practices" in 1907 to his valedictory Moses and Monotheism in 1939. Religion also constituted the principle theme of The Future of an Illusion and received major attention in Totem and Taboo. It was alluded to in the other works with which this study is concerned, as well as in other papers. From analysis of these writings on religion several propositions emerge:

1. Religion represents a response to man's feelings of weakness in the face of awesome

natural forces, his own physical frailty, and the frightening prospect of death.

2. Religion developed out of the original act of patricide, the resultant guilt and subsequent development of totemism.

3. God is a reflection of the father. This association developed out of the experiences of the early patriarchal human groups and man's inherited memories of such groups.

4. Religion domesticates the aggressive instincts which might otherwise jeopardize social cohesion.

5. Religion provides man a basis for morality.

6. Religious sentiment constitutes a wish-fulfillment; it has the character of an institutionalized neurosis and has been a socially necessary illusion.

7. Mankind might now be better off without religion. Reason and the reality principle should replace it.

Nature in its various manifestations confronted man with its awesome power. Man, by contrast, felt weak and helpless. Man evolved a coping mechanism built initially upon a foundation of animism, a primitive type of magical thinking. This involved belief in a world filled with "good" and "wicked" spirits which animated both natural forces and human beings. On the level of individual libidinal development animism manifested the individual's narcissistic (self-centered) stage. Religion developed out of animism as man humanized nature. The prototype of the man-nature relationship was the small child's helplessness vis-a-vis the father, upon whose protection he also counted. Thus the uncanny forces which had so dominated his existence were humanized and their appeasement became more possible. Anxiety was lessened.

Religion corresponded to that next stage of libidinal development when narcissism gave way to object relations, that of child to parent. The forces of nature were likened to beings whom men then turned into fatherly gods. The scientific stage which, for the greater numbers of people, still lay in the future would have an exact counterpart in the stage at which an individual has reached maturity, has renounced the pleasure principle, adjusted himself to reality and turned to the external world for the object of his desires.[42]

In time men observed that natural phenomena operated in a lawful manner. Nevertheless, man's memories of his childish helplessness and the memories of the childhood of the human race meant the longing for fatherly gods continued unabated. The affective significance of religious doctrines maintained its hold. In a remark strikingly similar to Marx's reference to religion as the "opiate of the masses" Freud commented that "the effect of religious consolations may be likened to that of a narcotic . . . ."[43] Myths, religion and morality all represented attempts to compensate for the uncertainty surrounding the gratification of human wishes.

[M]an's helplessness remains and along with it his longing for his father, and the gods. The gods retain their threefold task: they must exorcise the terrors of nature, they must reconcile men to the cruelty of Fate, particularly as it is shown in death, and they must compensate them for the sufferings and privations which a civilized life . . . has imposed on them.[44]

Death posed special problems for men. A corpse was an object of fear and dread. Extinction of the individual was difficult to comprehend so the deceased was conceived as the continued habitat of some remnant of the departed. But this ghost was capable of inflicting harm on those who had been ambivalent toward him in life. God could extricate man from this bind. The image of the omnipotent and omniscient father of childhood, invoked by acts of submission and renunciation, would be rewarded by God the father's protection and the possibility of eventual overcoming of the personal extinction of death.

Over each one of us there watches a benevolent Providence . . . . Death is not extinction . . . but the beginning of a new kind of existence . . . . In the end all good is rewarded and all evil is punished, if not actually in this form of life then in the later existences that begin after death. In this way all the terrors, the sufferings and the hardships of life are destined to be obliterated. Life after death . . . brings us all the perfection that we . . . missed here. And the superior wisdom [and] infinite goodness . . . are attributes of the . . . father who had all along been hidden behind every divine figure as its nucleus . . . . Now that God was a single person, man's relations to him could recover the intimacy and intensity of the child's relation to his father.[45]

The attempt to come to terms with death had other far-reaching implications. These included development of a mind-body dualism, the conception of immortality, reconciling man to the privations of earthly existence, and the generation of morality.

The changes wrought by death suggested . . . disjunction of the individuality into a body and a soul . . . . The enduring remembrance of the dead became the basis for assuming . . . life continued after death.

[M]uch later . . . religions devised the view of this after-life as the more desirable, the truly valid one, and degraded . . . life . . . to a mere preparation . . . . all with the purpose of [denying] death . . . as the termination of life.
Beside the corpse of the beloved were generated . . . a great part of man's deep-rooted sense of guilt [and] the earliest inkling of ethical law. The first and most portentous prohibition of the awakening conscience was: Thou shalt not kill. It was born of the reaction against that hate-gratification which lurked behind the grief of the loved dead . . . . [46]

Freud here provided in primitive form a social construction of religion. However, he ascribed a psychological imperative to this development, "man's deep-rooted sense of guilt." This is consistent with Freud's basic orientation which assumed a pathological basis to social constructions. Social sources for construction of religious thought, e.g., man's quest for community did not occur to him.

Freud's speculations concerning the primal horde and totemism were linked with, and proved a fertile source of ideas about religion and the development of morality. At time of publication of Totem and Taboo (1912) an active interest in totemism existed. Emile Durkheim's The Elementary Forms of the Religious Life appeared the same year. Durkheim asserted that in totemism all religions shared a common ancestry. Freud apparently read this work but referred to it in Totem and Taboo only in passing. However, as previously indicated, Freud acknowledged a number of ethnological and other sources including Sir James Frazer of Golden Bough fame and the psychologist, William Wundt who also wrote of totemism in 1912. Totem and Taboo thus reflected a contemporary trend in which scholars representing various disciplines viewed totemism as a "decisive phase in a hypothetical reconstruction of the [religious] history of mankind."[47]

Freud was struck by the correspondence between the two essential taboos of totemism, viz., the injunction against killing the totem and the prohibition against sexual relations with any woman belonging to the same totem, and the two salient features of the Oedipus complex, killing the father and "marrying" the mother. Equating totem animal and father provided an explanation for totemism and exogamy as institutionalized arrangements for overcoming the basic Oedipal drives toward parricide and incest. The totem feast ritually reenacted the Oedipal fantasy from man's prehistoric past. This feast commemorated the act from which emanated man's sense of guilt for original sin. Ultimately the figure of the murdered primal father was elevated from totem animal to deity.

> Totemism, with its worship of a father substitute, the ambivalency towards the father which is evidenced by the totem feast, the institution of remembrance festivals and of laws the breaking of which is punished by death--this totemism . . . may be regarded as the

earliest appearance of religion in the history of mankind, and it illustrates the close connection existing from the very beginning of time between social institutions and moral obligations.[48]

Freud likened the Christian ceremony of holy communion with its incorporation of the substance of the Redeemer to the content of the totem feast. Communion, however, emphasized the worshipful rather than the aggressive component of the old totem ceremony. Nevertheless, the ambivalence characterizing the father-son relationship is reflected in this religious ceremony.

> Meant to propitiate the Father Deity, it ends by his being dethroned and set aside. The Mosaic religion had been a Father religion; Christianity became a son religion. The old God, the Father, took second place; Christ, the Son, stood in his stead, just as in those dark times every son had longed to do.[49]

Christ represents both the resurrected Moses and the returned primeval father of the horde now transfigured from father to son.

In _Totem and Taboo_ Freud first advanced his view of guilt as the normal attitude of the individual toward all authority. Guilt is our inextinguishable social heritage with which religion attempts to deal. All religions are reactions to the original patricide with which "civilization began and which, since it occurred, has not allowed mankind a moment's rest."[50] Religion, through supplications to a forgiving authority, serves to relieve the sense of guilt. It retains its authority through monopoly of the ceremonial repetitions of the patricidal act, e.g., the Christian communion. Morality, also, is a response to guilt. The social and religious significance of guilt follows this Freudian formula: society was

> based on complicity in the common crime; religion was based on the sense of guilt and remorse attached to it, while morality was based partly on the exigencies of this society and partly on the penance demanded by the sense of guilt.[51]

Mankind's ethical systems had in part a rational basis, the necessity of delineating mutual rights and obligations in the interests of social stability. However, they were endowed with normative force by virtue of their connection with religion as an expression of the will of the father. Thus something grandiose and inevitable was imparted to the pragmatic aspect of morality. The gods represented cultural ideals in that every unattainable or forbidden wish was attributed to them.

Freud's writings reiterated that a progressive renunciation of pleasure-oriented drives was essential to civilization. The various religions played their role in effecting instinctual repressions. For example, certain acts were reserved to divinity.

> 'Vengeance is mine, saith the Lord.' In the development of the ancient religions . . . many things which mankind had renounced as wicked were surrendered in favour of the god, and were still permitted in his name; so that a yielding up of evil and asocial impulses to the divinity was the means by which man freed himself from them.[52]

Thus spake Freud in a 1907 paper. He continued the theme twenty years later in <u>The Future of an Illusion</u>. His Hobbesian view of man as an innately savage creature paves the way for the necessary restraining influence of morality rooted in religion. The prohibition of murder was again a case in point.

> When civilization laid down the commandment that a man shall not kill the neighbor whom he hates or who is in his way or whose property he covets, this was clearly done in the interest of man's communal existence, which would not otherwise be practicable. . . . Insecurity of life . . . now unites men into a society which . . . reserves to itself the right to . . . killing. . . .
> But we do not publish this rational explanation of the prohibition against murder. We assert that the prohibition has been issued by God.[53]

The trouble with this culturally functional solution to the problem of latent social violence is that, said Freud, it depends for its efficacy upon a continuing belief in God. What happens if (when?) this belief suffers erosion? Freud's supposition was that when the uneducated masses learned God did not exist only the force of the state could prevent general blood-letting. The only alternative would be a fundamental re-ordering of the relationship between civilization and religion.

Freud regarded religious belief as an institutionalized form of neurosis. Reading the ethnologist authorities of his day Freud was struck by the parallels between primitive populations and the contemporary neurotics whom he treated. Both shared a dread of incest. Also there existed a similarity between the irrational character of primitive taboos and neurotic phobias, and there was the same omnipotence of thought (equivalence of thought and deed) in primitive magic rituals and neurotic fantasies. The common factor, it appeared to Freud, was the murder of the primal father and the working out of the Oedipus complex. The ritualistic behavior of the individual suffering an obsessional neurosis, and religious rituals, derive from a common psychic source: the need to cope with pervasive ambivalence and a powerful, though unconscious, sense of guilt.

> [R]eligious phenomena are to be understood only on the model of the neurotic symptoms of the individual . . . as a return of long-forgotten important happenings in the primeval history of the human family, [and] they owe their obsessive character to that very origin and therefore derive their effect on mankind from the historical truth they contain.[54]

Although there was some question whether a universally held belief could be characterized as delusional, religion certainly represented an illusion, a substitution of a wish-fulfillment in lieu of reality. Freud distinguished "illusion" from "delusion" by describing the former as a

> belief [in which] a wish-fulfillment is prominent in its motivation, and . . . we disregard its relation to reality,

just as the illusion itself sets no store by verification.[55]

Religious ideas, therefore, contain both wish-fulfillment and significant historical memories (murder of the primal father/God). Religion is the universal obsessional neurosis of mankind. As with the obsessional neurosis of children, it arose out of the Oedipal involvement with the father and the necessity of warding off repressed wishes connected with this complex.

> We know that a human child cannot successfully complete its development to the civilized stage without passing through a phase of neurosis . . . . This is because so many instinctual demands which will later be unservicable cannot be suppressed by the rational operation of the child's intellect but have to be tamed by acts of repression. . . .
>
> [D]evout believers are safeguarded in a high degree against the risk of certain neurotic illnesses; their acceptance of the universal neurosis spares them the task of constructing a personal one.[56]

In Freud's dichotomous model the neuroses represent attempts to find _individual_ solutions for the problem of dealing with unsatisfied wishes, while societal institutions provide _social_ solutions to the same problems.

Institutionalized religion had also been established to help man achieve renunciation of his asocial and antisocial impluses.

> The structure of a religion seems . . . to be founded on the suppression or renunciation of certain instinctual trends; these trends are . . . egoistic, antisocial instincts, though even these for the most part are not without a sexual element. The sense of guilt in consequence of continued temptation, and the anxious expectation in the guise of fear of divine punishment, have indeed been familiar to

> us in religion. . . . [However] the suppression active in religion proves here also to be neither completely effective nor final. Unredeemed backslidings into sin . . . give rise to a new form of religious activity, namely, the acts of penance of which one finds counterparts in the obsessional neurosis.[57]

The fact religion constituted an illusion did not minimize its importance. Religious beliefs had served to comfort and console men and religion had performed a tremendous service for human civilization by curbing the instincts. But, Freud noted, this was no longer enough to justify its perpetuation. Far from eradicating mankind's psychic discomfort religion maintained its influence by fomenting an ever growing sense of guilt. Was it not time for men to be educated to reality? Would it not be better to ascribe purely rational reasons to the precepts of civilization, to derive them from social necessity?

> It would be an advantage to leave God out and . . . admit the . . . human origin of all the . . . precepts of civilization. Along with their pretended sanctity, these commandments and laws would lose their rigidity. . . . People could understand that [laws and regulations] are made, not so much to rule them as . . . to serve their interests. . . . this would be an important advance [toward] becoming reconciled to the burden of civilization.[58]

The struggle for self-mastery and against natural forces must in time find its base in reason and science. The latter was the key to knowledge of the real world. The final court of appeal must be reason. Only scientific work will provide reliable supports to reality. Almost polemically Freud pleaded the case for irreligiosity: Humble acquiesence in man's insignificance is "irreligious in the truest sense of the word."[59]

The decline of religious belief already was in process. Men must embrace reason or be suppressed by the state lest loss of faith cause loss of impulse control. No one could foresee how men raised without traditional religion would turn out. But, unlike the doctrinal rigidities of religion, the scientific approach ought to be modifiable in the light of experience. In any case,

> The whole thing [religion] is so patently infantile, so foreign to reality, that to anyone with a friendly attitude to humanity it is painful to think that the great majority of mortals will never be able to rise above this view of life.[60]

Freud's vision of the sweep of historical change was essentially positivist. His own time represented the third and last evolutionary stage. First there had been societies of primitive men unified through shared taboos; this was succeeded by a culture whose coherence was maintained by theological authority; now modern civilization held sway. The old system of morality was steadily weakening but had not yet been replaced by a new system of control. The marked prevalence of neuroses in contemporary civilization was connected with the interregnum in which a normative authority had not yet been reestablished. Religion was losing its hold and private neurosis (the "religion" of the individual) was replacing it. The proliferation of sects was another phenomenon reflecting the waning influence of traditional religion.

With the comment, "But surely infantalism is destined to be surmounted. Men cannot remain children forever. . . . ",[61] Freud cast his lot with the social evolutionists, with their nineteenth century faith in the idea of progress. Through an inexorable natural law of development, religion had guided men through their infancy; but, sharing Comte's belief in the ultimate triumph of science and reason, Freud felt relgion would "wither away" as it lost its hold on a maturing mankind. Nevertheless, such a victory would be a qualified one.

Could the masses of men achieve such rationalism? No, according to Freud. Replacing religious motives with secular ones could be accomplished only by the cultured elite. The masses would remain inherently hostile to culture and amenable to social control only through the authority of traditional beliefs. The masses' awareness of rationalist thought would not likely produce the necessary changes toward scientific habits of thinking. Learning that God did not exist might make them feel exempt from the rules of civilization with consequent unleashing of egoistic and aggressive drives. Therefore, religion needed defending as a socially functional illusion. The fact God is a hoax must be concealed. Comte recognized the social utility of religion; so did Durkheim and Karl Mannheim. The latter's interest in creation of a "'faith' appropriate to our time"[62] testified to the social need of some form of uncritical belief.

Freud shared with William James a belief that the variety of relgious experiences masked an underlying unity. Freud's interpretation, however, differed from James'. The uniformity is not in the identity of the object experienced but in the common human needs of the experiencing subjects. Religious belief has its genesis in the elaboration to a societal level of the child's relationship to his parents. Infantile dependency is a culture-free universal. It is this invariant which is abstracted from diverse patterns of family relationships and made the prototype of religious "truth."

Freud's critique of religion poses a challenge to religious orthodoxy. The religious view sees conscience as an active agent of rapprochement with the eternal, i.e., culturally autonomous, verities. For Freud the child acquired a conscience through internalizing parental controls, which induced socialization to extant social authority. Freud's position that conscience stems from parental and social authority suggests a rigidity of conscience structure and function. This supports his extrapolation of society as the family writ large and seems to invite two empirical errors: 1. Conscience has been known to deviate from its original model and to evolve in response to later experiences; 2. Freud assumed a consistency in the ethical injunctions provided the child by his various role models. Freud apparently failed to allow for variations in behavior and in moral prescriptions offered by significant others. He also underestimated the ability of the young to judge and discriminate. Considering them <u>tabulae rasae</u> was inconsistent with the empirical orientation with which Freud had pursued his clinical efforts.

Freud assumed a dichotomy between the educated elite and the masses in their attitudes toward religion: rejection by the former and credulity by the latter. This seems markedly over-generalized, certainly in relation to the contemporary situation. Lack of belief transcends class lines; so does fidelity to religious dogma. Freud's equating of religious orthodoxy with divinely legitimated authority over-simplified religion by ignoring distinctions between religion as faith and religion in its institutionalized forms. Freud made no distinction between the churches and Christianity. In <u>Group Psychology and the Analysis of the Ego</u>, and elsewhere, Freud used the Catholic church as his model of religious authority and orthodoxy. As a Viennese, he saw the church as a familiar symbol. The model of hierarchical authority was evident. As a member of a "despised minority" Freud resented the institutionalized religious orthodoxy which cast aspersions on the "non-faithful."

Freud also overlooked the fact that rationalist "science" with its value-free ideology can become not a liberating force but an instrument of social control. On the other hand, its forerunner, religious sentiment, can be critical of the status quo. This offers an ironic twist to Freud's belief in the evolutionary trend toward rational criticism of society.

On the whole Freud's assessment of religion seems one-sided in its emphasis on the repressive nature of this instituion. His view that religion helps maintain social order (a position in accord with Durkheim's) leaves no room for what manifestly has been an aspect of the western religious tradition. From the Hebrew prophets' denouncing the iniquities of the rich and powerful, to the Roman Catholic hierarchy's efforts to help desegregate public schools in the American south, religion has also represented a force for social change.

Rieff notes that Freud did recognize that the interpretation of behavior, the "definition of the situation," was affected by situational referrants. Thus

> while today 'neuroses appear in a hypochondriachal guise, masked as organic diseases . . . the neurosis of

olden times masqueraded in demonological shape.'[63]

Freud failed to allow for the transformation of meaning when an individual act is performed in public or expresses a socially approved motive. This point was central to Durkheim's thought on religion.

Durkheim, like Freud, believed a rationalist explanation of religion was altogether inadequate. For Durkheim, the most important quality of religion is its function in making life endurable. This is not far from Freud's position. Durkheim believed it is the reinforcement the worshipper receives from the communion with other believers, the drawing from the strength of the collectivity in its acts of worship and its professions of faith, that is essential to religion's strength. Religion, above all, is a collectively experienced event. The religious rite makes the person a member of the community as well as validating his affiliation with the special group. The strength of the community is a buffer against whatever evil may beset the person and it ushers him into the presence of death under the most supportive circumstances. This essential communality was not an aspect of Freud's thought on religion. It may be that his grounding of behavior within an essentially individualistic framework extending outward, rather than from collective to individual, caused him to miss this point.

Durkheim traced religion to the community itself and the elevation of its authority to the level of the sacred. Freud traced religion to a much more circumscribed origin, as has been discussed. Durkheim saw religion in its essential character as indestructable. The forms and symbols varied with time and with different groups but not the collectivity's need for reaffirmation of itself and its togetherness. Freud saw at least the potential for discarding what he perceived as a remnant of man's childhood. He did not recognize its reappearance in less explicitly religious terms, such as in his own psychoanalytic movement with its "priesthood" of analysts and cult of believers.

Table 1, on the following page, represents a comparison between Freudian and Durkheimian[64] thought along several dimensions related to religion.

TABLE 2

SELECTED ASPECTS OF RELIGION AS CONCEPTUALIZED BY FREUD AND DURKHEIM

Concept	Durkheim's Thought	Freud's Thought
Original Form of Religion	Totemism	Totemism
Significance of Totem Animal	Objective representation of the social order Precursor of God	Feared and venerated primal father through whom primal crime is expiated and remembered. Precursor of humanized god
Nature of God	Society elevated to sacred status	A transformation of the primeval father remembered because of inherited memory traces; also represents the father of the person's family of origin.
God's Time Frame	God endures because he symbolizes the collectivity (society), which is immortal.	God endures because of invariant psychosocial constellations which generate the Oedipus complex; man's longing for authority makes God forever necessary.
Religion's Relation to Human Morality	Morality is the "collective representation." Religion verifies and strengthens the normative structure.	Man committed "original sin" with the first act of patricide. Religion a means of expiation, and curbs "wickedness" (asocial and antisocial drives).
"Function" of Religion	Makes life more endurable; solidifies social relationships.	Relieves sense of guilt; restrains aggressive impulses.
Locus of Social Control	Society, sui generis	Society itself as coercive authority; super-ego as an internalized control stemming from parental (Father/God) identification.
Religion's Future	Indispensable as a cohesive force; coextensive with society itself.	Questionable. Elite minority may outgrow religion in favor of scientific rationalism; masses may continue to need religion to assure conforming behavior.

Religion: Beyond Freud and Durkheim

Durkheim's <u>Elementary Forms of the Religious Life</u> and Freud's <u>Totem and Taboo</u>, each dealing with the origins of the religious impulse, were published in the same year, 1912. While Durkheim laid down the functionalist sociological approach to religion, a more contemporaneous sociological view would complement his "response" to Freud on this subject.

Freud (and Comte) to the contrary notwithstanding, it seems likely religion would survive the advent of a scientific world view. This is because, building upon Durkheim's ideas, several social functions of religion have been identified which provide it a durable place in human societies. Religion functions as a social glue by uniting a community of believers whose shared rituals bind them with shared values and beliefs. Religion also provides the individual emotional support in the face of some of the great traumas of earthly existence (as Freud affirmed). In addition, life would be far more difficult to bear without the sense of meaning and purpose to life which religion provides. Moreover, religion reinforces important societal norms which, through their investment with sacred meaning ("Thou shalt not kill") strengthen the legal code and the edifice of social control. Finally, religion sanctions, and supports people through, the rites of passage. Certain transitions in the life cycle, of which marriage is a good example, are essential to society's perpetuation. Endowing these with a sacred quality strengthens their role and significance.

Finally, regardless of the ultimate ascendancy of a scientific world view, science must remain mute concerning the ultimate, transcendental questions: What are the purpose and meaning of life? Traditional allegiance to a church-centered religion may decline but not the need for the sacred and supernatural in the life of mankind.

NOTES

[1] The "group" to which Freud referred in this work covered a wide spectrum, including a "crowd" and both small and large formally organized entities. Freud used the army and the Catholic church as his principal illustrative examples.

[2] Sigmund Freud, Group Psychology and the Analysis of the Ego, Standard Edition, XVIII, 1968, p.70.

[3] Sigmund Freud, Totem and Taboo, Standard Edition, XIII, p. 157.

[4] Sigmund Freud, Moses and Monotheism (New York: Random House, 1939), p. 120.

[5] Sigmund Freud, Group Psychology and the Analysis of the Ego, op. cit., pp. 73, 74.

[6] Sigmund Freud, Moses and Monotheism, op. cit., p. 125.

[7] Ibid., pp. 127, 128.

[8] Sigmund Freud, Group Psychology and the Analysis of the Ego, op. cit., p. 103.

[9] Ibid.

[10] Ibid., p. 118.

[11] Sigmund Freud, Totem and Taboo, op. cit., p. 74.

[12] Ibid., p. 72.

[13] Jacob Arlow, The Legacy of Sigmund Freud (New York: International Universities Press, 1956), p. 87.

[14] Sigmund Freud, Group Psychology and the Analysis of the Ego, op. cit., p.88.

[15] Ralph Turner, "Collective Behavior," in Robert E. Faris, ed. Handbook of Modern Sociology, (Chicago: Rand-McNally, 1964).

[16] Sigmund Freud, Moses and Monotheism, op. cit., p. 129.

[17] Ibid., pp. 139, 140.

[18] Paul Roazen, Freud: Political and Social Thought (New York: Alfred A. Knopf, 1968), p. 221.

[19] Sigmund Freud, Group Psychology and the Analysis of the Ego, op. cit., p. 91.

[20] Ibid., pp. 42, 43, 44.

[21] Ibid., p. 116. Italics in the original.

[22] Ibid., p. 105, et seq.

[23] Sigmund Freud, Civilization and its Discontents, Standard Edition, XXI, 1968, p.114.

[24] Sigmund Freud, Moses and Monotheism, op. cit., p. 153.

[25] "Civilized Sexual Morality and Modern Nervousness," (1908) in Sander Katz, ed., Freud: On War, Sex and Neurosis, trans. by Joan Riviere, et al., (New York: Arts and Science Press, 1947), p. 167.

[26] Sigmund Freud, "Thoughts for the Times on War and Death," Freud: On War, Sex and Neurosis, op. cit., pp. 254,255.

[27] Sigmund Freud, Civilization and its Discontents, op. cit., p. 132.

[28] "Thoughts for the Times," op. cit., pp. 252, 256, 275.

[29] Erving Goffman, The Presentation of Self in Everyday Life, (Garden City, New York: Doubleday, 1959).

[30] Erik Erikson, Identity and The Life Cycle (New York: International Universities Press, 1959).

[31] Sigmund Freud, Civilization and its Discontents, op. cit., p. 101.

[32] Ibid., p. 104.

[33] Ibid., pp. 103, 104.

[34] Ibid., pp. 104, 105.

[35] Ibid., p. 103.

[36] Sigmund Freud, "Family Romances" (1908), in Standard Edition, IX, p. 237.

[37] Nancy Chodorow, The Reproduction of Mothering (Berkeley: University of California Press, 1978), p. 178.

[38] Ruth Benedict's Patterns of Culture (New York: Penguin Books, 1934) represented an early attempt by modern anthropologists to document family structural diversity and the varied patterns of intra-familial conduct in different cultures.

[39] Jonathan Glover, "Sigmund Freud, Morality and Responsibility," In Jonathan Miller, ed., Freud: The Man, His World, His Influence (Boston: Little, Brown and Company, 1972), p. 153.

[40] Kenneth Burke, A Grammar of Motives (Berkeley: University of California Press, 1969), pp. 430, 431.

[41] Sigmund Freud, Group Psychology and the Analysis of the Ego, XVIII, op. cit., 122.

[42] Sigmund Freud, Totem and Taboo, XIII, op. cit., p. 90.

[43] Sigmund Freud, Future of an Illusion, op. cit., p. 49.

[44] Ibid., pp. 17, 18.

[45] Ibid., p. 19.

[46] Sigmund Freud, "Thoughts for the Times on War and Death," Freud: On War, Sex and Neurosis, op. cit., pp. 269, 270.

[47] Henri F. Ellenberger, The Discovery of the Unconscious (New York: Basic Books, Inc.), p. 895.

[48] Sigmund Freud, Moses and Monotheism, op. cit., p. 105.

[49] Ibid., p. 111.

[50] Sigmund Freud, Totem and Taboo, op. cit., p. 145.

[51] Ibid., p. 146.

[52] Sigmund Freud, "Obsessive Actions and Religious Practices" in Freud: On War, Sex and Neurosis, Sander Katz, ed., trans. by Joan Riviere, et al (New York: Arts and Science Press, 1947), p. 145.

[53] Sigmund Freud, Future of an Illusion, op. cit., p. 31.

[54] Sigmund Freud, Moses and Monotheism, op. cit., p. 71.

[55] Sigmund Freud, Future of an Illusion, op. cit., p. 31.

[56] Ibid., pp. 42, 43, 44.

[57] Sigmund Freud, "Obsessive Actions and Religious Practices," op. cit., pp. 143, 144.

[58] Sigmund Freud, Future of an Illusion, op. cit., p. 41.

[59] Ibid., p. 33.

[60] Sigmund Freud, Civilization and its Discontents, op. cit., p. 74.

[61] Sigmund Freud, Future of an Illusion, op. cit., p. 49.

[62] Philip Rieff, Freud: The Mind of the Moralist, op. cit., footnote, p. 294.

[63] Sigmund Freud, "A Seventeenth-Century Demonological Neurosis" (1923), quoted in Rieff, op. cit., p. 289.

[64] Emile Durkheim, The Elementary Forms of Religious Life, trans. by Joseph W. Sivain (Glencoe, Illinois: The Free Press, 1947).

CHAPTER VI

SIGMUND FREUD AS SOCIAL THEORIST

The present chapter concludes this essay on Freud's social thought. The first section discusses the general applicability of Freud's ideas to social science and the extent to which these ideas retain contemporary relevance.

Freud, Biological, Psychological, and Social Man

The history of science is replete with ideas which won recognition only belatedly (e.g., the germ theory of disease), and with ideas winning uncritical acceptance only to be abandoned later (e.g., Mesmerism). Sigmund Freud's ideas seem to have survived the faddism which characterized their early reception in the United States. Now psychoanalysis as a body of thought, seems to be experiencing an outcome paralleling other innovative systems: some parts have largely been discarded (e.g., the death instinct), some adopted in such explicit form as to bear the founder's name (e.g., the Freudian slip), some modified to the point of distortion (e.g., the sexual instinct as the basis of all human behavior), some absorbed so subtly and completely as to create indelible cultural change while losing all traces of paternity. Concerning the last-named, David Bakan commented, "The far-reaching consequences of Freud's thought are paradoxically confirmed by the degree to which his contributions are taken for granted."[1]

Nevertheless, Freudian thought has on the whole encountered considerable resistance from social scientists. At the time Freud's ideas first were penetrating the American intellectual market (about the second decade of this century) sociology had its own agenda. The positivistic emphasis was coming to the fore. Stress was placed on the acquisition of data through quantitative methods. Freud's wide-ranging generalizations, which offered no empirical data acquired under carefully controlled conditions, seemed anti-scientific. Moreover, Freud's grim and unrelenting view of man may not have fit well with the "upbeat" view of man held by sociologists still under the influence of the liberal Protestant ministry which had been so influential in forming sociology's value base. Also, such early works as Totem and Taboo seemed more related to areas of interest to anthropologists. Perhaps most important, one of the founding fathers, Durkheim himself, had laid down in Rules of the Sociological Method that the appropriate unit of analysis for sociology was not the individual, but the collectivity. Freud's focus was regarded as psychological reductionism, flawed by preoccupation with the irrational and lacking stable situational referrents.

To explore the rise and proliferation of psychoanalytic thought during its founder's own lifetime might require an essay in the sociology of knowledge. Here can only be noted briefly the fact, as Galdston[2] has pointed out, that a number of Freud's discoveries already had been identified in some form by Romantic medicine, i.e., during a period preceding Freud. Galdston states unequivocally that psychoanalysis could not have been conceptualized before the latter part of the nineteenth and the early part of the twentieth century. Only after medicine had been fragmented and led away from its human component by the influence of French rationalism and the school of Helmholtz, was a revolution possible re-orienting medicine to the study of man and his subjectively experienced growth and development. This Freud achieved. Whatever criticism may be leveled at Freud's thought as psychological reductionism, it is nevertheless true that Freud's genius led the way toward a modern conceptual framework in which man is studied "holistically," both in the natural and social sciences.

This holistic conception also provided medicine and psychiatry, and then social science, with an awareness that the total field of human behavior involved dimensions larger than the conscious and the cognitive. Meaning and purpose had to be understood on more than one level of awareness. This principle applied from the earliest dyadic relationship, i.e., from early infancy, onward. Moreover, the ascription of meaning extended through the entire range of behavior, to include both "normal" and "abnormal." These were not discrete entities but existed on a continuum. Otherwise, Erving Goffman would hardly have chosen Asylums as a proper setting for a study of rule making and social interactions.

Freud's contribution, that social behavior may have functions of which participants are consciously oblivious, both complicates and profoundly enriches the study of human behavior. "Man does not live by bread alone" takes on added depth of meaning. Certainly a psychoanalytically oriented sociology cannot be expected to redirect its attention from the interactions occuring in the socially constructed "real" world. To do so would mean abandoning the sociological perspective. However, the mental dynamisms unearthed by Freud, which help people organize their psychic realities, also help to explain how "public acts" (social institutions and social rules) become private realities. Interpenetration of the macro-processes of society and the micro-processes of individual behavior is effected through both cognitive and affective processes, and Freud called particular attention to the latter.

Two of the most important of the mental dynamisms are identification and sublimation, both of which have been discussed in this study. Each operates to renew and extend the individual's commitment to the continuity of the culture. Identification helps explain the working of the socialization process in family life, in peer and work groups, etc. Freud called attention through identification, to why the individual wishes to learn what he needs to learn. Thus socialization is a cognitive and value-building process resting upon a powerful affective foundation. Sublimation makes possible the redirection of "private affects" which may, in their inception be socially divisive, into socially sanctioned, "culture building" activities. Freud seemed to recognize that specific cultures shaped drive expression toward their own ends. He seemed not to be aware that identification and sublimation were devoid of any meaning without the assumption of a pre-existing social reality in which these processes could unfold. Nevertheless, Freud has extended our understanding of the way culture is transmitted though the identificatory process.

Talcott Parsons may be the most notable sociological theorist to acknowledge a debt to Freud.

His attempt to reorder functionalist theory stipulated that social action and symboling involve both cognitive <u>and</u> affective components.[3] Indeed, as Martindale notes, "Parsons turns to Freud . . . for a theory of personality adequate for functionalism."[4] Another theorist of functionalism, Robert Merton[5] has applied Freud's conception of manifest and latent content of ideas, to manifest and latent functions in the operation of social systems. Thus subterranean channels of communication or of need fulfillment may make a system viable, although these covert elements are not (except under sociological analysis) recognized to be structurally related to the system.

In 1930 Freud received the Goethe prize, Germany's foremost award for literary distinction. Freud was a gifted and persuasive writer. His mode of thought was couched in the scientific imagery of nineteenth century physics-- suppression of forces, displacement, etc.--but it also was rich in literary references and historical and philosophical allusions, and he made vivid and imaginative use of metaphor and analogy. Thus the superego was likened to a garrison within an occupied city. Indeed, Jerome Bruner says Freud was not a theorist in the conventional sense; rather, his mode of thought was "a metaphor, an analogy, a way of conceiving man, a drama . . . . Freud is the ground from which theory will grow."[6]

These literary qualities make interesting reading but pose difficulties in analysis. It is not possible always to know when Freud literally meant what he said and when he was speaking only metaphorically. Sometimes Freud warned the reader that only an analogy was involved, but he was not always consistent. For instance, Freud first introduced the idea of the primal horde in <u>Totem and Taboo</u> (1912). He amassed an extensive body of citations from the ethnological literature out of which he developed his own modified version of the alleged event. Then he used it to deduce a number of his major theoretical positions concerning the origins of religion, the family, and social organization. He reintroduced the primal horde in <u>Group Psychology</u> (1921) but this time he referred to Darwin's idea as a "conjecture" and added,

> to be sure, this is only a hypothesis, like so many others with which archeologists endeavor to lighten the darkness of prehistoric times--a

'Just-So Story,' . . . ; but I think it is creditable to such a hypothesis if it proves able to bring coherence and understanding into more and more new regions.[7]

Here Freud apparently regarded the primal horde idea as of essentially heuristic value. But then in Civilization and its Discontents (1930) the concept was reintroduced and discussed in several places[8] without qualifications concerning its literal veracity. In Moses and Monotheism (1939) Freud acknowledged that

> more recent ethnologists have without exception discarded [the primal horde hypothesis but] . . . I still adhere to this sequence of thought.[9]

It seems Freud wished to have it both ways. As was indicated in chapter V, the essence of the primal horde concept, i.e., its value in representing (symbolizing) the historical reality of a modal type of nineteenth century family life, establishes its validity for analytic purposes, not anything else.

Freud's penchant for analogies extended to dreams and myths. The former expressed infantile wishes, the latter the residues of a people's childhood. Individual fantasies and national myths were analogized. The fantasies became group constructions which then appeared as myths, legends, and fairy tales. Social life was replete with symbols, indeed was organized in terms of symbols which disguised the origins of certain social relationships and masked their inner meaning.

Participant observation as a method for "getting into" another frame of reference may well provide insights otherwise unobtainable. Freud's clinical work was, of course, a form of participant observation. As an "anthropologist" of the neurotic Freud's use of analogies may have possessed some utility. He analogized incompletely socialized child, neurotic and savage. However, the repeated use of analogies for purposes of generalization suggests reification. It undermines Freud's claim to a scientific approach and suggests the appellation social critic rather than social scientist may more accurately reflect his role.

Among contemporary sociologists, and also a user of participant observation is Erving Goffman, himself an employer of the analogical strategem. Goffman is a master at seeing through the deception games and dissembling which go on behind face-to-face encounters.[10] Roles are strategies, life is a game of "Will the real self please hide out." If Freud could be said to have a sociological heir, Goffman might be the logical candidate for investiture.

Early in Freud's career he did notable work in neurology. Though he subsequently abandoned efforts to find physiological origins for psychological processes, he used biological propositions to help account for cultural developments. Some of these propositions are of dubious validity. One such is the doctrine of recapitulation, which Freud applied extensively. Recapitulation (ontogeny recapitulates phylogeny) was based upon the resemblance between successive forms which the maturing embryo passed through en route to its final form. The evolutionary transformation of the species thus was presumed to be recapitulated in the development of the individual embryo. Freud believed that the principle extended to psychological development as well. Indeed, he asserted, there were living fossils in the form of primitive peoples whose culture and mental processes were rudimentary forms of later, more advanced forms (viz., European peoples).

Freud believed the growth of mind in the child recapitulated that of the "savage." The individual Oedipus complex recapitulated events which had transpired in the primeval family. Moreover, Freud conceived the primitive, infantile, and archaic as co-existent with the civilized and the evolved in the human mind.

> In the realm of the mind . . . the primitive mind is . . . commonly perceived alongside the transformations which have developed out of it . . . . Nothing once formed in the mind can ever perish, . . . everything survives in some way or other, and is capable under certain conditions of being brought to light again . . . . [11]

Two important implications of Freudian thought derive from this. One involves Freud's acceptance of a Lamarckian position: acquired characteristics can be inherited. The sense of guilt persisting from the time of the primal parricide was a case in point. Freud acknowledged the general lack of support for his Lamarckian position. Nevertheless, he held to this view. It remains a minority stance, drawing support only from the fringes of ethnology.[12] Freud's premise of invariant psychological processes operating independently of social variables is dealt a serious, if not fatal blow by this stubborn fact: demonstrable proof of the inheritance of acquired characteristics is lacking.

The second difficulty concerns Freud's belief in a process of unilinear evolution, the fountainhead of which was the decisive act of primal parricide which forever changed human society. Freud accounted for obvious divergences in cultural practices by stipulating differences in levels of evolutionary development attained by various societies. Contemporary "primitives" were at the evolutionary level of civilized man's ancestors. Freud's concept of "primitive man" has long since given way to that of "preliterate man" and invidious comparisons have been abandoned by most students of human behavior. Such socially interacting variables as demographic changes, the prevailing technology, availability and type of natural resources, patterns of communication, the nature and extent of culture contact, etc., seem more adequately to account for differences among societies than do fixed biological differences leading to a fixed unilinear development common to all mankind. Social scientists have abandoned attempts to develop a theory of social origins. The variables are too manifold, the data base nonexistent.

One way of stating the difference between psychoanalytic and sociological perspectives is to say that Freudian man is driven by inner forces while sociological man seeks to establish, and accommodates to, rules for the conduct of human interaction. Freud's explanatory paradigm "psychologizes" man, leading to a consistent attribution of behavior to innate maturational patterns and psychic residues which encounter a coercive and limiting social environment. Thus social reality is essentially derivative, a product of internal forces. This intrinsic and "stage" approach to the study of human behavior projects the characteristics of individuals onto the external world. Such reductionism makes more difficult the task of synthesizing psychoanalytic and social constructs. This is particularly evident if Freudian thought is extended to its logical conclusion, which is that culture is alien to man, imposed upon resisting and unhappy individuals. So stated, the position is anti-sociological.

Yet Freud also displays a certain ambiguity. Consider the Oedipus complex. In order for the complex to ripen, a sequence of psychosocial developments must occur based upon the child's intensive interactions with nurturing adults. Resolution of the complex through substitution of identification for ambivalent rivalry with the parent of the same sex involves interpersonal transactions, not merely biological processes. Moreover, Freud's delineation of these transactions has added an important dimension to the sociological view of the family. Thus Freud re-enters (in spite of himself, one is tempted to say), the company of social interactionists.

In the primary sources drawn upon in this study Freud provides further evidence he is aware that social reality is implicated in the development and functioning of the individual. In <u>Group Psychology and the Analysis of the Ego</u>, Freud commented,

> In the individual's mental life someone else is invariably involved, as a model, as an object, as a helper, as an opponent; and so from the very first individual psychology . . . is at the same time social psychology as well.[13]

Freud's view of the ego was consistent in seeing its differentiation from the id, and its growth, as a process mediated by the continuing influence of the outer world. The superego was a product of incorporated parental standards, modified subsequently by societal standards. In <u>The Future of an Illusion</u> Freud acknowledged the importance of the social environment.

> [T]he mutual relations of men are profoundly influenced by the amount of instinctual satisfaction which the existing wealth makes possible.[14]

156

Freud's relegation of women to an inferior position is widely recognized and may readily be documented in his writings. Nevertheless, here too, he called attention to the significance of the environment: "We must beware . . . of underestimating the influence of social customs which . . . force women into passive situations."[15] And in reporting one of his famous early cases ("Dora"), Freud remarked,

> it follows from the nature of the facts which form the material of psychoanalysis that we are obliged to pay as much attention in our case histories to the purely human and social circumstances of our patients as to the somatic data and the symptoms of the disorder.[16]

But these ideas are almost asides and are not systematically developed. They temper but do not invalidate the essential criticism that Freud typically focussed upon a rather narrow band of the behavioral spectrum.

Freud's characteristic perspective points up another limitation in his social thought. This is his uncritical assumption of a unilateral association between human needs and values in which needs constitute the independent variable. However, a social science perspective would suggest that, excepting basic physiological needs--food, air, and water--the reverse may be true; i.e., values may determine needs. For instance, the value of "achievement" generates the "need" for competition. Basic societal values define needs, which come to be regarded as inherent. The sources of the values themselves would appear to reside in social structural conditions. The social relations generated by the private enterprise system produce the familiar competitive-acquisitive orientation with its valued type: economic man, for whom the market mentality, thrift, acquisitiveness, possessions, the performance ethic are, in the revealing phrase, "second nature," i.e., taken for granted as "natural." Freud seemed to disdain contemporary society while regarding its institutions--family, religion, etc.--as largely reflective of innate dispositions (needs). The relentless analyst of the psyche who took nothing for granted about the individual human heart took a great

157

deal for granted when it came to the social institutions in which these individual psyches played out their lives.

And yet--once again--another look at Freud's reductionism may be indicated. If psychologism is one-sided, so may be "sociologism" and Freud's emphasis on the innate in man may prove useful to social science, after all. What Freud did with his insistence upon man's innate biologically derived character was to remind sociologists that, as Lionel Trilling in eloquent, though rather mystical language, put it,

> Somewhere in the child, somewhere in the adult, there is a hard irreducible, stubborn core of biological urgency, and biological necessity, and biological reason, which culture cannot reach and which . . . sooner or later . . . will . . . resist and revise [the culture].[17]

Trilling's point is that there is a residue of human quality beyond the reach of cultural control which is capable of standing aloof from the culture, as it were, and criticizing it and preventing its absolute control over human behavior. Trilling asserts that Freud's emphasis on biology is a liberating idea in its resistance to and modification of cultural omnipotence.

Dennis Wrong makes a similar point when, as he so forcefully puts it,

> In the beginning there is the body . . . . As soon as the body is mentioned the specter of 'biological determinism' raises its head and sociologists draw back in fright. And certainly their view of man is sufficiently disembodied and non-materialistic to satisfy Bishop Berkeley, as well as being desexualized enough to please Mrs. Grundy.[18]

Wrong responds to sociologists who criticize Freud as too biological by pointing out that

When Freud defined psychoanalysis as the study of the 'vicissitudes of the instincts,' he was confirming, not denying, the 'plasticity' of human nature insisted on by social scientists.[19]

Wrong also believes sociologists misuse Freud's concepts of internalization and the superego by employing them to explain social order and stability. Internalization of the norms does not assure conformity, only the development of guilt over nonconformity. As Freud pointed out, those with the strongest conscience experience the greatest guilt and conflict. Norm violaters require external coercion because they have not fully internalized a superego, hence do not experience enough guilt. Wrong adds, "To Freud man is a social animal, without being entirely a socialized animal."[20]

Rebellion indeed may be precipitated by biological imperatives. On the other hand, it may also be a function of identification with models who themselves are innovators and rebels; it may be a response to conditions generally perceived as depriving or unjust, etc. Thus motivations toward nonconformity can have cultural antecedents, after all. Hence, the aptness of Wrong's argument may be conceded without negating the continued relevance of the social context.

Thus Freud has influenced sociologists to enlarge their conception of socialization. As indicated in the discussion of the Family in Chapter V, Freud had pointed out that for some people conforming behavior is a matter of expedience, not inner conviction; acquiesence to the norms follows from "dread of . . . community" sanctions, rather than integration with community standards. "Good" behavior does not signify respect for legitimate authority but a pragmatic recognition of the power of the institutions of social control. However, just as such "undersocialization" is possible, so is "oversocialization." An instance of the latter would be a Weberian "ideal type," come to life in the robotic, bureaucratic servant who obeys the rules in a "not to reason why" fashion.

Some of the undersocialized become the very models of overt conformity but seethe with inner discontent. The widespread existence of covert norms juxtaposed with the ideal ("official") norms indicates the tensions existing between these polarities of social behavior. Goffman's work has explored this realm of unease in social life.

Freedom and Necessity in Freud's Thought

Determinism is the position that present behavior is totally a consequence of previous behavior and past circumstances. Rather logically, the idea tends to be associated with macro-theories. As such a system theorist, Marx stipulated that the "kingdom of necessity" (monopoly capitalism) would yield to the "kingdom of freedom" (classless communism). He thereby extricated his own "ism" from the freedom/necessity dilemma without, however, bothering to share the petty details of how this was to be accomplished. Freud developed a system which he specifically disclaimed to be a Weltanschauung, claiming psychoanalysis aspired only to the world-view espoused by science. Nevertheless, the question of determinism in Freud's thought needs to be addressed.

Freud was dedicated to a deterministic frame of reference. The mental universe operated lawfully. Utilitarian ideas were prominent in his thinking, i.e., the Benthamite notion that behavior was directed toward attainment of pleasure and avoidance of pain. The implications of Freud's approach to causation were teleological, containing an implicit fatalism. One reading of Freud, therefore, suggests that indeed necessity has won the day. Man was doomed by his act of "original sin"--the primal parricide--to repetitive symbolic reenactment of this event in his family of orientation, just as a coercive society was mandated by man's unquenchable aggression.

Here again, however, the richness of Freud's thought reveals a two-sided coin. To begin with, the concept of causality in psychoanalysis clearly represents a logical principle. Empirical generalizations are not inherently necessary. Causality, however, is an assumption requisite to the scientific method.

Freud's social thought illumines the issue of freedom versus causal explanation. "Psychic determinism" meant for him that all behavior was meaningful, not arbitrary or random. It did not mean everything could be causally explained. The fact a behavioral event has causes does not imply that it had to occur, that the actor was locked into an inevitable sequence of following events. Discovering causes for events made possible effective intervention in the causal chain. Clearly, psychoanalysis had this very purpose and its assumptions supported the idea that things need not endlessly repeat themselves. Freud also made the same point in The Future of an Illusion. He felt this essay might help some people realize the limitations of unthinking, dogmatic religious faith.

When Freud said, "Where id was, there ego shall be," he qualified his determinist position ierrevocably, for he asserted the primacy of the intellect, of reason, even if such a triumph did not occur very often. Unquestionably, Freud saw man as conditioned and limited by his own biological heritage (reflected in the id), by his cultural history and social circumstances (reflected in the superego). Man in society will always be subject to tensions, conflict, and ambiguity. Learning to live with these consituted an awareness of human necessity and in this very awareness lay a degree of freedom.

There is even a pragmatic basis for believing that Freud, in spite of his "biologism," fundamentally believed in the triumph of freedom over necessity. Freud's life and work testify to this. His dedication to psychoanalysis meant that he was committed to a belief in the human capacity for change. His reflections on his own life supported this position. He had mentioned in his Autobiographical Study that he had developed "a certain degree of independence of judgment" based upon his marginal position as a Jew in a hostile Gentile environment (cited in Chapter II, page 27). Freud was a person of penetrating intellect, wide learning, tenacious self-discipline, and a relentless drive for achievement. He mobilized these qualities to overcome barriers of ethnicity and depreciated social status. The intellectual ferment and change he stimulated show how far beyond "necessity" his system of thought carried his own and subsequent generations.

Individual and Society: Freud and Parsons

Talcott Parsons believed that Freud's ideas about "object-relations" provided a means for integrating psychoanalytic personality theory and sociological theory about structure and functioning of social systems. The interpenetration between the bounded organism and the external world occurred when the sociological construct of role was related to Freud's concept of "relational needs," i.e., the child's need for love. The pleasure principle of the child's personality system "meets" the reality principle of the social system via contact with parents, the "agents" of the social system.

> The point to emphasize is that the most crucial part of 'reality' even at the oral level is social; it is the mother as a social object, acting in a role in a system of social interaction. . . .
>
> [The infant] learns to play a social role in interaction with the mother. . . . Together . . . mother and child come to constitute a collectivity in a strict sociological sense. . . .
>
> [T]he process of ego development takes place through the learning of social roles in collectivity structures.[21]

Parson's subsequent comment seems close to G. H. Mead's thinking.

> [B]y internalizing the reciprocal role-interaction pattern [the child] lays the foundation of capacity to assume alter's role as well as his own.[22]

Parsons makes a further point. He regards Freud's theory of object-relations as

> essentially an analysis of the relations of the individual to the structure of the society in which he lives. Freud analyzed this relationship from the point of view of the individual rather than . . . the social systems concerned. His perspective also was primarily developed in the psychological sense; sociologically stated, he was mainly concerned with the processes by which the individual . . . acquire[s]

membership in social collectivities, to learn to play roles in them, and to internalize their values, and he was most interested in the identifications entered into in early childhood.[23]

Parsons' observations raise two points, both of which prompt questions about his analysis. The first concerns Freud's apparent failure to realize the full sociological implications of the resolution of the Oedipus complex. While the child succeeds in internalizing the normative structure as it exists in the parent, neither Freud nor Parsons seemed to recognize the further consequences of this fact. Parental erotic solidarity forces the child to turn to the larger, extra-familial society. Here further value modification and instrumental learning are acquired. Other institutions of society--first school, then the economic system--become accessible, because the child has been freed by the defeat of his Oedipal aspirations. He now can effect engagement with these other social systems. Freud (and Parsons) however, seemed to stop with the child's internalization of parental norms.

The second point is related to the first. Parsons seems to have "tamed" Freud, the conflict theorist. The former's analysis suggests that the early object-relations which lead to role competence succeed in creating a stable, fully socially integrated person. This may support functionalist theory, but it does not altogether do justice to Freud's position.

Alvin Gouldner supports this criticism when he asserts that men's sentiments may be at variance with what he calls their "domain assumptions," i.e., the prevailing normative structure. This dissonance requires that the functionalist perspective in sociology, of "a sculptural Appolonian ideal of man as firmly bounded and contained, as temperate and restrained"[24] must be rejected. The spectrum of reality, he goes on to say, is not encompassed by conformity and non-conformity but must include active opposition to societal rules. Individualization and opposition to conformity are as human as the quest for consensus.

Individual and Society: Freud and the Family

In his essay, "Civilized Sexual Morality and Modern Nervous Illness," Freud discussed the opposition between the needs of civilization and the needs of sexuality. In asserting the primacy of society (or civilization, as he referred to it), Freud also asserted the protection of the individual. For one, relinquishing of individual aggression safeguarded the existence of each, while the incest taboo promoted wider social units and social cooperation against the threat of family domination. But the defense of society also meant the defense of civilization's achievements against the individual, who was required to sacrifice his personal gratification for "higher" values. Gerald Izenberg correctly describes Freud's assessment as "a characteristic ambivalence between individual autonomy, on the one hand and social harmony and higher values, on the other."[25]

Freud's ideas about personality formation were rooted in mid-nineteenth century family structure and roles and his ambivalent view of society and the individual's place in it followed from this. He identified the superego as the internalized representation of the father who embodied authority and represented society and its norms to the child. This family structure reinforced patriarchal authority and tradition. Freud recognized that, at the same time, ambivalence and opposition necessarily were generated because unquestioning obedience to the father inevitably conflicted with the need for autonomy, in order to compete successfully in the market place.

These contradictory demands were embodied in ego and superego and

> were particularly characteristic of the traditional family in Germany and Austria. . . . If to these factors are added the increasing political exclusion and decreasing prestige of the liberal bourgeoisie in the Austro-Hungarian Empire, and the particular situation of the Jewish father, who demanded respect at home but had none in the streets,* one has a set of conditions in which it was possible to distance oneself

sufficiently from paternal authority to examine it consciously while yet realizing its effective importance.[26]

*Recall the incident, vividly remembered by Freud, when his father meekly submitted to insult from a Gentile on the streets of Vienna. (Noted in Chapter II).

Marx and Freud: The Mode of Production and the Mode of Reproduction

This study has indicated how markedly influential Darwinian thought was for the development of Freud's ideas. That other towering nineteenth century figure, Karl Marx, apparently went unnoticed by Freud. However, in a number of ways the Marxist and Freudian orientations form an interesting complementarity, to the exposition of which this study now turns.

Freud was twenty-seven and barely launched on his medical career when Marx died in 1883. Neither Freud nor his biographers mention Marx as a theorist of whom Freud was cognizant. However, Freud shared with Marx several characteristics, and their overlapping lives meant they also were exposed to certain prevalent intellectual influences. Each was influenced by Enlightenment thought so that rationalism and a materialist and deterministic outlook characterized their thought. Thus each considered religion a species of fraud. Both shared a conviction that surface phenomena reflect underlying objective laws of development. Each developed a theoretical system linked to practice--revolutionary activity for Marx, psychotherapy for Freud. Each undertook the role of social liberator, Marx probably more self-consciously so by exhorting mankind to develop awareness of historic forces in order to control them. Freud's message was less explicitly stated and more oriented toward the individual than toward a social class. The individual can "liberate" himself through achieving conscious understanding of his own psychodynamic processes ("where id was, there ego shall be"). But this liberation is not possible for the masses of mankind, as Marx thought. Only the elite, like Plato's philosopher-kings, were capable of achieving dominion over the unruly passions of the self. For most of mankind society would exercise a repressive and constraining function. There were several reasons:

1. Social life cannot be maintained without the subordination of individuals' pleasure-seeking impulses. This thesis Freud developed in Civilization and its Discontents.

2. Conformity to the demands of civilization exacts a heavy psychic toll on all but the relatively few educated intelligent, and constitutionally capable of thoroughly sublimating their aggressive drives.

3. Man's innate aggressive impulses express a natural, unavoidable intra-species conflict and are a manifestation of the death instinct which finds expression in wars. The pacifist, Freud pointed out to Einstein in "Why War?", is found only among the intellectually emancipated, biologically superior minority. The superior individual can sublimate aggressive drives into creative achievements in the realms of art, science, literature, etc. The outlookd for civilization is hardly sanguine.

Freud's theory of society thus took as a given the idea that society is inherently repressive, not expressive. Although Freud recognized the compelling power of love in human relationships, he never extrapolated this awareness to a societal level. Had he done so he more likely than not would have recognized that society not only constrains but literally humanizes, enriches and enables the members of the collectivity.

Freud also assumed as self-evident a division of mankind into those capable of surmounting their biological heritage, capable of converting the unavoidable frustrations of social life into high achievement, and those incapable of accomplishing this. Concerted human activity to transform society into a less constraining configuration occurred to Marx. It did not occur to Freud for whom the capitalist, patriarchal and stratified society of his time was natural and ineluctable. Freud's patients were no more trapped by their psychic compulsions than was their physician by his own ethnocentrism.

Freud, in the tradition of Hobbes, Locke, and Rousseau, saw society as an artifact developed out of the self-interest of individuals. A compact assuring order protected members of the group. In thus hypothesizing society as an aggregate of independent individuals who come together out of calculated utilitarian motives Freud's thought is ultimately rooted in a psychological base. In this respect Freud and Marx represent polarities of thought while holding in common the rationalism of the Enlightenment and the idea of progress. Social evolution is implicit in the grand design and can be realized through bringing social forces (Marx) or human nature (Freud) under conscious control.

Darwin's Origin of Species had demonstrated to Freud that the human species had evolved ("progressed"), even as August Comte's positive philosophy had, even earlier, anticipated societies' evolutionary ascent to a scientific mode of thought.

Freudian and Marxist thought are compared and contrasted in Table 2 on the following pages.

Selfhood, Authority, and the Social Compact

The Marx/Freud table has pointed up how strongly individualistic and therefore how removed from the sociological Freud's thought appears to be. Nevertheless, the centrality of conflict in Freudian thought focuses attention upon the element of the social implicit in his thought. Robert Bierstedt says this clearly and incisively:

> It is in this contrary juxtaposition of id and superego that the awareness of self arises and it is this conflict that gives us our conception of it. It is in the repression of impulse that we become conscious of the fact that there is something else in the universe than ourselves, and it is this consciousness that gives us also the sense of self.

> There are thus certain similarities in the theories of Cooley, Mead, and Freud. All three, however different their intellectual orientations, arrive at a theory of the self that requires society. For none of the three is self-consciousness possible without the presence, and, in one case the

TABLE 2
A COMPARISON OF FREUD AND MARX ON SELECTED DIMENSIONS OF THEIR THOUGHT

Dimension of Social Thought	Marx	Freud
Intellectual Influences on His Thought	Romanticism in its emphasis on the integrated wholeness of an integrated society. The Enlightenment with its rational, deterministic outlook. The Hegelian dialectic of change.	Romanticism in its emphasis on the significance of affect and inner feelings. Enlightenment thought: rationality and determinism. Darwinian thought with its emphasis on intra-species conflict.
General Theoretical Orientation	Conflict Theorist: contending social classes. Social Evolutionist: movement toward a classless society Anti-idealist	Conflict Theorist: individual contending with self; individual contending with a suppressive society Social Evolutionist in Comtean sense: movement toward a society based on science. Anti-idealist
Theorist's locus of Concern	Man's exploitation of man. Contemporary society oppresses and alienates man and must be changed	Man's inner conflicts. Society frustrates man, particularly in his sexual expressiveness.
Nature of Individual's Relationship with Society	Human beings are innately social. Man never existed in a "state of nature." The social entity is prior to the individual.	Human beings are innately individualistic. The male sexual drive, female need to nurture and child's need of love and protection create families. Society a construct designed to control and channel outward, innate aggressive drives which otherwise would destroy men and lead to dominance of brute force.

TABLE 2 (continued)

Dimension of Social Thought	Marx	Freud
		Sexuality and social life exist in opposition because former tends to exclude other relationships. Society constrains, therefore is experienced by most men as psychically burdensome.
The "Independent Variable" in Social Structure	Social relationships generated by prevailing mode of economic production determine class relationships, the person's social position, and the existing ideology. Social forces (primarily opposing class interests and developing "contradictions" in socioeconomic conditions) produce conflict and change. The times produce the man to lead the way to the new social synthesis.	Man's sexual and aggressive drives caused the primal parricide, the consequences of which led to establishment of social order and such institutions as religion, the patriarchal, exogamous family, etc. Heroic men of great intellect and driving will dominate their times.
Ideological Superstructure	The ruling ideas of a society are the ideas of the ruling class, although people believe themselves to be acting and thinking freely. Ideas, values, norms are epiphenomena of the underlying foundation of socioeconomic relationships.	People believe themselves to be autonomous and rational but their conscious mentation is influenced by unconscious processes. Man is both the rational and rationalizing creature. Cultural attainments--artistic creations, scientific thought, etc. are produced by sublimation of the erotic and aggressive drives.

TABLE 2 (continued)

Dimension of Social Thought	Marx	Freud
Significance of Conflict	Conflict is part of the dynamic of history, socially generated by competing class interests. It will cease with achievement of the classless society.	Intra-species conflict natural to life forms, including man. Conflict therefore a characteristic of individuals. Men are in conflict with their own impulses which socialization has caused them to curb or reject, and with the society which demands restraint as the price of protection from mutual destruction.
Attitude Toward Religion	Religion a device to lull men to quiescence. Religion perpetuates social oppression by providing ideology justifying existing institutional arrangements.	Religion is an illusion, a projection of the need of a father-figure, to allay feelings of weakness and guilt over sexual and aggressive drives.
Significance of Work	Under capitalist mode of production work is an alienating activity. In the future society men will no longer be alienated from products of their labor and work will again be a creative and self-fulfilling enterprise.	The mature person can love and work. For most men work is onerous and they work only because they must.
Alienation	Man is alienated from himself by conditions of capitalist production and exploitive social relationships.	Neurotic individuals, appearing in increasing numbers, are self-alienated by id and superego conflicts (instinctual demands vs. cultural prohibitions). Unless

TABLE 2 (continued)

Dimension of Social Thought	Marx	Freud
Social Stratification	Owners of means of production wield power because of economic wealth and control of political process and propaganda. Stratification has existed in every previous society except for primitive communism. Communism will finally end differential distribution of rewards and power.	sublimation can be achieved culture increases man's burden of guilt and unhappiness. Stratified societies inevitable and necessary because of inherent qualitative differences between people. Great men rule as exemplifications of the father. Women's subordinate position reflects their intellectual and characterological inferiority to men.
Approach to Effecting Social Change	Key to change lay in reordering the material world, thus an action-oriented approach. Men must demolish the existing order not "by mental criticisms . . . but only by the practical overthrow of the actual social relations . . . ."	Key to change lay in transformation of the individual. Talk had the potential for effecting change. This could lead to mastery of inner drives.
Dynamics of Social Evolution	Human societies engaged in uni-linear progress toward a classless Utopia. Men's developing consciousness of their own interests would move the evolutionary process forward.	Human societies had progressed from an animistic stage to a religious stage. A scientific stage would follow in which rationality would govern men's behavior. Whether the masses of men could attain this level was problematic. The primal parricide (Freud's version of "original sin") had never been expunged from men's inner awareness, hence a utopian

TABLE 2 (continued)

Dimension of Social Thought	Marx	Freud
		state was unlikely. Probably only the intellectually elite could forego the illusion of religion and adopt a scientific orientation.
Valued Social Goal	Establishment of a conflict and alienation-free society.	Development of a conflict-free individual, integrated and self-aware. "Ordinary unhappiness" would replace neurotic misery.

repressions of society. Thus . . . we
have a view of the self that is
explicitly sociological. The individual
has a self only because he first
acquires a society.27

In Freud's conception the invariable concurrence
of order and conflict in societies reflected the
dualism in individual development. The first tie in
the miniature society of the family is that of
authority. Parental dominance and its reciprocal, the
love of the child for his parents, precedes the
struggle for Oedipal gratification which culminates in
an act of renunciation, again a deference to
authority. However, the tie to authority arises prior
to relations involving erotic feelings. Hence social
compliance antedates the formation of moral ideals.

In Group Psychology and the Analysis of the Ego
Freud distinguished between "sexual" and "social"
emotions, i.e., "object-love" as contrasted with
"identification-love." Again priority belonged to the
relation to authority. Two types of love are
established. The first concerns what one would like
to have (object-love) and the other, initially that of
a child for its parents, is what one would like to be
(identification). "[I]dentification is the earliest
and original form of emotional tie."28 It develops
prior to sexuality and stems from submission to
parents. It is the model of all internalized
authority. Legitimated authority figures--teachers,
leaders, etc.--apart from social sanction also depend
upon the implicit mechanism of identification. Freud
connected love with authority by asserting that the
"so-called identification" not the "object cathexis"
explains social cohesion. The political leader exerts
authority by "putting himself in the place of the
subject's parents,"29 thereby evoking the earliest
form of love.

Darwin's adoption of the idea of survival of the
fittest was consistent with the ideology of a
competitive free enterprise system; so may Freud have
adopted a variety of the Hobbesian solution to the
problem of social order stemming from his immersion in
and extrapolation of the bourgeois society of his
time. For Freud this society reflected human nature.
However, Freud's view of man and society was more
sophisticated than that of Hobbes. Freud also
recognized an inherent emotional community. Because

the infant's libidinal needs require gratification, love for and dependence upon parents develops, making man a social creature. He is born into the society of the family, a prototype (for Freud) of later and larger aggregates. Thus for Freud the Hobbesian view of society is incomplete. Social authority rests not just on force but on love as well.

Both Hobbes and Freud belong in the ranks of contract theorists because they hypothesized a compact which provided legitimacy to society. However, Freud did not confine his explanation strictly to rational motives, as did Hobbes. It was not just to ward off the dangers of anarchy but a response to the wish for authority, a "longing for the father"[30] who had been deposed (but not forgotten) at the time of the primal murder. Authority--in the horde, the family, the state--has the social function of limiting freedom. The concern that individual freedom and the social order are incompatible has been expressed by theorists from Plato to Marx. In thus equating authority with constraint Freud recognized a central dynamic of social change and social order. As authoritative institutions, e.g., the medieval church, lost authority, another social institution, the state, took its place. The contemporary family provides another example. As the authority of the family declines, its control over children's behavior is replaced by peer group norms. Authority as a central characteristic of social relations remains a manifest reality.

What appears lacking in this aspect of Freud's analysis is any reference to a variable complementary to authority. Men submit, but they also may choose. Social order is a function of constraint, but it also is a function of human reason. Cooperation in pursuit of rationally defined goals is a social reality, too. Freud simply may have neglected to explore the full implications of his own thought. Freud demolished the Rousseauean myth of a primal innocence corrupted by society. Infantile sexuality and the aggressive impulses of man's organic nature, while empirical realities, did not transform innocent individuals into perverted ones. Freud was neither a Rousseauean nor Hobbesian because he recognized that the self becomes socialized in the process of maturation. Along with the aggressive, "evil" impulses Freud recognized powerful forces capable of effecting repression and sublimation.

Thus the logic of Freud's thought, if not his language, suggests that human nature in its inception is both asocial and "neutral," and that society is the necessary matrix for achieving a fully human existence. Human behavior is organically conditioned but it is socially organized.

Sigmund Freud as Social Theorist

Sigmund Freud introduced a theory of human behavior which assumed a fundamental purposiveness to human actions. By implicating both conscious and unconscious sources of such action he brought the entire spectrum of behavior, "normal" and "abnormal" within the purview of scientific study. Thorstein Veblen had enlarged the concept of "economic man" by introducing non-economic motives into the study of economic behavior. Similarly, Freud enlarged the concept of social man by introducing psychological motives into the study of social behavior. Anthropology provides a good example of Freud's contribution. Prior to Freud explanations of the practices of pre-literate peoples were sought in "rational" motives: prestige, economic gain, etc. No recognition existed that social customs may have purposes of which the participants are consciously oblivious.

Freud's social essays, however, took the form of social philosophy and social criticism. Generalizing from his clinical discoveries he offered value judgments concerning contemporary western society, and he indicted prevailing norms of sexual behavior and religious belief. While offering sweeping generalizations about the origins of human society, the family, religion, and morality, Freud's writings failed to ground these ideas in any explicit social theory. Instead, individual human nature--aggressive and guilt ridden--provided Freud the grounding for his "theory" of social man. The postulates from which his social theory was elaborated were largely implicit. Extricating these from his essays provided the numbered statements presented at the beginning of Chapters IV and V. These reveal some of the major limitations of his social thought. These limitations have been discussed in the last three chapters of this study and will only be alluded to here.

Freud persistently believed in the Lamarckian theory of inheritance of acquired characteristics. This Freud extended to encompass mental reactions, including, most significantly, a primeval guilt. This inherited psychic burden helped account for morality, religion, and crucial interpersonal developments in family life. Thus the social heredity of Durkheim's collective representations was replaced by a literal biological heredity of remembered guilt.

Freud's social theory was individualistic both in its inception and elaboration. For instance, social groups were an outgrowth of individual libidinal ties originating in family life. Leaders were father representations who fulfilled individuals' needs for love and authority. The hierarchical structure of societies rested upon genetic inequalities and the innate neeed for authority felt by most individuals. The charismatic father figure was indispensable to social order. The collectivity consisted of the sum of its individuals rather than comprising an entity generating its own laws of development and behavior. Rooted thus in the psychodynamics of individual development, social institutions were assumed to possess qualities of universality and timelessness. Freud's individual was inevitably repressed, hence society was inevitably repressive. Thus culture represented a projection of the self; socialization was the analog of individual repression.

Freud's profoundly ahistorical viewpoint was paralleled by an equally deep-seated ethnocentrism. The base-line for comparative assessment remained the middle-class European male and his patriarchal family, circa 1885-1920. Thus committed, Freud perpetrated the error of generalizing about human societies from a patently unrepresentative sample of middle-class European neurotics.

Several additional observations complete this compendium of Freud's limitations as a social theorist. His model of normative functioning--the ability to love and to work--leaves out play, a characteristic of primate behavior. This seems a curious oversight for a student of man, though perhaps not so remarkable when Freud's personal dedication to work is recalled. In another notable omission Freud, the exponent of reason and intellect, finds little or no place for the cognitive in deriving and maintaining the social order. All, or almost all, is coercion and constraint. Freud observed that social institutions function as adaptive processes for dealing with commonly experienced psychological problems. He saw the social system as a collective defense against erotic and aggressive drives. However, this acute perception stopped short of any reference to the roles of human reason and cooperation in creating and maintaining these institutions. Indeed, Freud's intra-psychic and individualistic approach to social theory failed to incorporate in any systematic way a social level of reality.

In spite of these difficulties Freud's social thought does contain important insights, implicit and unsystematized though they may be. To begin with he stipulated that the developing human being possesses inherent libidinal needs whose satisfaction requires external "objects." These objects, i.e., people, reflect society's normative structure. The individual is assured provision of libidinal satisfactions conditional on his repressing normatively unacceptable impulses. Thus the self emerges as a social product, created out of repressions generated by the need to come to terms with the social world. Repressing unacceptable impulses imposes the social world on individual consciousness. To the growth and socialization of the cognitive self Freud thus added an affective, libidinal component.

This additional element powerfully expanded our understanding of socialization processes. Freud's recognition of the child's capacity for identifying with role models affirms an interactionist perspective in his thought. Also, he attempted to mesh biology and culture by integrating inner biologically given drives with "objects" representing the external world. Freud thus contributed his answer to the persistent Hobbesian question, "What is the basis of social cohesion and stability?" The individual internalizes the social order by incorporating a superego. External authority, represented by nurturing adults, is transformed into inner acquiescence.

Freud explained the individual's commitment to the continuity of the culture by offering a theory of initial socialization through the interactions of family life. Socialization "works" not only because of the child's conscious ideational learning but because of the authority structure of the family. Authority, Freud pointed out, is ubiquitous in the social structure and in social relationships. Power and constraint are acceptable trade-offs for most children in exchange for love and gratification. The redirection of sexual and aggressive drives is accomplished through processes Freud discovered: identification and sublimation. The former enables transmission of desired and appropriate behaviors; the latter enables redirection of sexual and aggressive drives into culture-building activities. Freud once again was addressing the interface between social acts, i.e., compliant behaviors, and private motives, i.e., the need for love and libidinal gratification. Thus, the interpenetration of the macro-processes of society and the micro-processes of individual behavior achieved concrete explication.

Sources of social scientists' reluctance to accommodate their ideas to Freudian thought have been identified earlier in this chapter. An additional element appears to be the fact that Freud kept the door open for reconsideration of man as, after all, still a biological organism. However, for social science the implications of biological man seem of considerable import. An irreducible core of organicity exists in man; hence his behavior cannot adequately be studied without recourse to a more comprehensive paradigm than contemporary social theory can offer. This more inclusive model would encompass both the cognitive stressed by sociology, and the affective areas of human behavior. To some extent this already has happened through the general acceptance of Freud's postulate concerning existence of purpose and intention extending through the gamut of human behavior. Thanks to Freud the "irrational" has entered the purview of scientific study.

Freud hypothesized a coercive social structure. This held in check both overt and latent aggression from those incapable of sublimation, and those with superego deficiencies, i.e., the undersocialized. Freud recognized empirically the existence of the latter, who obeyed the rules out of practical regard for the power of social sanctions. By conceptualizing such socialization processes as identification and superego formation, Freud provided a theoretical base to help account for this phenomenon of undersocialized man.

Freudian thought represented man as that eminently irrational creature who may, after all, be studied, comprehended, and influenced by a rationally devised science of his own creation, psychoanalysis. This is perhaps the most interesting paradox in a system of thought rich in paradoxes. Much of Freud's impressive legacy of thought has been absorbed into our enduring cultural heritage. Much of it was flawed. Many of the implications of Freud's thought await further study and ultimate comprehension. If his social thought has not now achieved the universal validity Freud's ambition sought, nevertheless it has expanded our horizons.

NOTES

[1] David Bakan, *Sigmund Freud and the Jewish Mystical Tradition* (Princeton: D. Van Nostrand Co., Inc., 1958),p. 4.

[2] Iago Galdston, "Freud and Romantic Medicine," *Bulletin of the History of Medicine*, XXX, 1956, reprinted in *Freud: Modern Judgments*, Frank Cioffi, ed. (London: Macmillan, 1973), pp. 103-123.

[3] Talcott Parsons, Robert F. Bales, and Edward A. Shils, *Working Papers in the Theory of Action* (Glencoe, Illinois: The Free Press, 1953), pp. 31, 36.

[4] Don Martindale, *The Nature and Types of Sociological Theory* (Boston: Houghton Mifflin Co., 1960), p. 495.

[5] Robert F. Merton, *Social Theory and Social Structure*, rev. ed. (Glencoe, Illinois: The Free Press, 1957), p. 51.

[6] Jerome Bruner, "Freud and the Image of Man," *Partisan Review*, (Summer 1956), reprinted in Frank Cioffi, ed., *Freud: Modern Judgments*, (London: Macmillan Press, Ltd., 1973), p. 145.

[7] Sigmund Freud, *Group Psychology and the Analysis of the Ego*, Standard Edition, XVIII, p. 122.

[8] Sigmund Freud, *Civilization and its Discontents*, Standard Edition, XXII, pp. 100, 101, 131, 132.

[9] Sigmund Freud, *Moses and Monotheism*, trans. by Katherine Jones (New York: Random House, Inc., 1939), p. 169.

[10] Erving Goffman, *Encounters*, (Indianapolis: Bobbs-Merrill, 1961).

[11] Sigmund Freud, *Civilization and its Discontents*, op. cit., pp. 68, 69.

[12] Desmond Morris, The Naked Ape (New York: McGraw-Hill, 1967).

[13] Freud, Group Psychology and the Analysis of the Ego, op. cit., p. 69.

[14] Sigmund Freud, The Future of an Illusion, Standard Edition, XXI, p. 6.

[15] Sigmund Freud, New Introductory Lectures on Psychoanalysis: Standard Edition, XXII (London: The Hogarth Press, 1933), 116.

[16] Ernest Jones, The Life and Work of Sigmund Freud, Vol. III, (New York: Basic Books, Inc.), p. 336.

[17] Lionel Trilling, Freud and the Crisis of our Culture (Boston: The Beacon Press, 1955), p. 54.

[18] Dennis Wrong, "The Over-socialized Conception of Man in Modern Society," American Sociological Review, Vol. 26, No. 2, April 1961, p. 191.

[19] Ibid., p. 192.

[20] Ibid.

[21] Talcott Parsons, "Social Structure and the Development of Personality," Psychiatry, November 1958, pp. 327, 328, 329.

[22] Ibid., p. 329.

[23] Ibid., p. 338.

[24] Alvin W. Gouldner, The Coming Crisis of Western Sociology (New York: Basic Books, Inc., 1970), p. 427.

[25] Gerald N. Izenberg, The Existentialist Critique of Freud (Princeton: Princeton University Press, 1976), p. 65.

[26] Ibid., pp. 330, 331.

[27] Robert Bierstedt, The Social Order, 3rd ed. (New York: McGraw-Hill Book Co., 1970), p. 193.

[28] Sigmund Freud, Group Psychology and the Analysis of the Ego, Standard Edition, XVIII, op. cit., p. 107.

29Ibid., p. 127.

30Sigmund Freud, <u>Totem and Taboo</u>, Standard Edition, XIII, p. 148.

SELECTED BIBLIOGRAPHY

Freud's Works Reviewed for this Study
(Listed in order of original publication, by date)

Books

Totem and Taboo [1912], The Standard Edition of the Complete Psychological Works of Sigmund Freud, Trans. under the general editorship of James Strachey in collaboration with Anna Freud assisted by Alix Strachey and Alan Tyson, London: Hogarth Press, 24 Vols., Vol. XIII, 1955.

On the History of the Psychoanalytic Movement [1914], Standard Edition, Vol. XIV, 1968.

Group Psychology and the Analysis of the Ego [1921], Standard Edition, Vol. XVIII, 1968.

An Autobiographical Study [1925], Standard Edition, Vol. XX, 1968.

The Future of an Illusion [1927], Standard Edition, Vol. XXI, 1968.

Civilization and its Discontents [1930], Standard Edition, Vol.XXI, 1968.

New Introductory Lectures On Psychoanalysis [1933], Standard Edition, Vol. XXII, 1968.

Moses and Monotheism [1939], trans. by Katherine Jones, New York: Random House, 1939.

An Outline of Psychoanalysis [1940], Standard Edition, Vol. XXIII, 1968.

The Origins of Psychoanalysis: Letters to Wilhelm Fliess, Drafts and Notes: 1887-1902, Bonaparte, Marie; Freud, Anna; and Kris, Ernst, (eds.), trans. by Mosbacher, E. and Strachey, J. New York: Basic Books, 1954.

Letters of Sigmund Freud. Freud, Ernst L., ed., trans. by Stern, Tania and James, New York: Basic Books, 1960.

The Freud/Jung Letters. McGuire, William, ed., trans. by Mannhein, Ralph and Hull, R.F.C. Princeton: Princeton University Press, 1974.

Articles
(Listed in order of original publication, by date.)

"Obsessive Actions and Religious Practices [1907], Freud: On War, Sex and Neurosis, Katz, Sander, Ed., trans. by Riviere, Joan and Strachey, John. New York: Arts and Science Press, 1947.

"Civilized Sexual Morality and Modern Nervousness," [1908], Freud: On War, Sex and Neurosis, Arts and Science Press, 1947.

"Family Romances" [1908] Standard Edition, Vol. IX, 1959.

"The Origin and Development of Psychoanalysis," American Journal of Psychology, Vol. 12, 1910, pp. 181-218.

"The Claims of Psychoanalysis to Scientific Interest" [1913], Standard Edition, Vol. XIII, 1955.

"Thoughts for the Times on War and Death" [1915], Standard Edition, Vol. XIV, 1968.

"A Seventeenth-Century Demonological Neurosis" [1923],Standard Edition, Vol. XIX, 1968.

"Why War?" [1932], Civilization, War and Death, Rickman, John ed., London: Hogarth Press, 1968.

"Address to the Society of B'nai B'rith" [delivered 1926; first published 1941], Standard Edition, Vol. XX, 1959.

Secondary Sources

Books and Dissertations

Alexander, Franz. Our Age of Unreason. Philadelphia: J. B. Lippincott Co., 1942.

Alexander, Franz and Selesnick, S. T. The History of Psychiatry. New York: Harper and Row, 1966.

Arlow, Jacob. The Legacy of Sigmund Freud. New York: International Universities Press, Inc., 1956.

Bakan, David. Sigmund Freud and the Jewish Mystical Tradition. Princeton: D. Van Nostrand Company, Inc., 1958.

Bandura, Albert. Aggression. Englewood Cliffs, New Jersey: Prentice Hall, Inc., 1973.

Barber, Bernard. Science and the Social Order. New York: Collier Books, 1962.

Benedict, Ruth. Patterns of Culture. New York: Pelican Books, 1946.

Betteridge, Harold D., ed. The New Cassell's German Dictionary, New York: Funk and Wagnalls, 1971.

Bierstedt, Robert. The Social Order, 3rd ed., New York: McGraw-Hill Book Co., 1970.

Brown, J. A. C. Freud and the Post-Freudians, Baltimore: Penguin Books, 1964.

Bruner, Jerome S. "Freud and the Image of Man" in Cioffi, Frank, ed. Freud: Modern Judgments, London: Macmillan, 1967.

Burke, Kenneth. A Grammar of Motives, Berkeley: University of California Press, 1969.

Cassirer, Ernst. The Philosophy of the Enlightenment, trans. by Koelln, Fritz and Pettegrove, James P., Princeton: Princeton University Press, 1951.

Chodorow, Nancy. The Reproduction of Mothering, Berkeley: University of California Press, 1978.

Cioffi, Frank, ed. Freud: Modern Judgments, London: Macmillan Press,1973.

Collins, Randall and Makowsky, Michael. The Discovery of Society, 2nd ed., New York: Random House, 1978.

Costigan, Giovanni. Sigmund Freud, New York: The Macmillan Company, 1965.

Cuzzort, R. P. and King, E. W. Humanity and Modern Sociological Thought, New York: Holt, Rinehart and Winston, 1969.

Decker, Hannah S. Freud in Germany, New York: International Universities Press, Inc., 1977.

Demerath, N. J., III and Peterson, Richard A., eds. System, Change and Conflict, New York: The Free Press, 1967.

DeTocqueville, Alexis. Democracy in America, Heffner, Richard, ed., New York: New American Library, 1961.

Durkheim, Emile. The Elementary Forms of Religious Life, trans. by Sivain, Joseph W., Glencoe, Illinois: The Free Press, 1947.

Ellenberger, Henri F. The Discovery of the Unconscious. New York: Basic Books, Inc., 1970.

Erikson, Erik H. Identity and the Life Cycle, New York: International Universities Press, 1959.

Fromm, Erich. Sigmund Freud's Mission, New York: Harper and Brothers, 1959.

Gay, Peter. Freud, Jews and Other Germans, New York: Oxford University Press, 1978.

Gerth, Hans and Mills, C. Wright,. Character and Social Structure, New York: Harcourt Brace, 1953.

Glover, Jonathan. "Freud, Morality and Rsponsibility," Jonathan Miller, ed., Freud: The Man, His World, His Influence, Boston: Little, Brown and Company, 1972.

Goffman, Erving. The Presentation of Self in Everyday Life, Garden City, New York: Doubleday, 1959.

Goffman, Erving. Encounters, Indianapolis: Bobbs-Merrill, 1961.

Gouldner, Alvin W. The Coming Crisis in Western Sociology, New York: Basic Books, Inc., 1970.

Grollman, Earl A. Judaism in Sigmund Freud's World, New York: Appleton-Century, 1965.

Gross, Llewellyn, ed. Sociological Theory: Inquiries and Paradigms, New York: Harper and Row, 1967.

Hinkel, Gisela J. The Role of Freudianism in American Sociology, unpublished Ph.D. Dissertation, University of Wisconsin, 1951.

Hollitscher, Walter. Sigmund Freud. London: Routledge and Kegan Paul Ltd., 1970.

Hollowell, A. I. "The Child, The Savage and Human Experience," In Proceedings of the Sixth Institute on the Exceptional Child, Langhorne, Pennsylvania: Child Research Clinic of the Woods School, 1939.

Izenberg, Gerald N. The Existentialist Critique of Freud. Princeton: Princeton University Press, 1976.

Jones, Ernest. The Life and Work of Sigmund Freud. 3 vols. New York: Basic Books, 1953-1955.

Kuhn, Manfred H. The Contribution of Sigmund Freud to Social Science: A Critical Analysis, unpublished Ph.D. Dissertation. University of Wisconsin, 1941.

Kuhn, Thomas. The Structure of Scientific Revolution, 22nd ed., Chicago: University of Chicago Press, 1970.

Landis, Bernard and Tauber, Edward S., (eds.). In the Name of Life: Essays in Honor of Erich Fromm. New York: Holt, Rinehart and Winston. 1971.

Lauzan, Gerard. Sigmund Freud. The Man and His Theories, trans. by Evans, Patrick, Greenwich, Connecticut: Fawcett Publications, Inc., 1965.

Levitt, Morton. Freud and Dewey on the Nature of Man. New York: Philosophical Library, 1960.

LeBon, Gustave. The Mind of the Crowd. New York: Viking Press, 1960.

MacIntyre, Alasdair. Herbert Marcuse. New York: Viking Press, 1970.

MacIsaac, Sharon. Freud and Original Sin. New York: Paulist Press, 1974.

Malinowski, Bronislaw. *Sex and Repression in Primitive Society*. New York: Harcourt, Brace & Co., 1927.

Marcuse, Herbert. *Eros and Civilization*. New York: Vintage Books, 1962.

Martindale, Don. *The Nature and Types of Sociological Theory*. Boston: Houghton Mifflin Co., 1960.

Mead, Margaret. *The Coming of Age in Samoa*. New York: William Morrow & Co., 1928.

Merton, Robert. *Social Theory and Social Structure*. Glencoe, Illinois, The Free Press, 1957.

Miller, Jonathan (ed.). *Freud the Man, His World, His Influence*. Boston: Little, Brown and Co., 1972.

Morris, Desmond. *The Naked Ape*. New York: McGraw-Hill, 1967.

Nelson, Benjamin (ed.). *Freud and the 20th Century*. Cleveland: World Publishing Co., 1957.

Nietzsche, Friedrich. *Genealogy of Morals*. Kaufman, Walter. *The Portable Nietzsche*. New York: Viking Press, 1954.

Nisbet, Robert. *The Social Philosophers*. New York: Thomas Y. Crowell Co., 1973.

Park, R. E. and Burgess, E. W. *Introduction to the Science of Sociology*. 2nd ed. Chicago: University of Chicago Press, 1924.

Parsons, Talcott; Bales, Robert F., and Shils, Edward A. *Working Papers in the Theory of Action*. Glencoe, Illinois: 1953.

Parsons, Talcott and Bales, Robert. *Family, Socialization and Interaction Process*. New York: The Free Press, 1955.

Parsons, Talcott. *Societies*. Englewood Cliffs, New Jersey: Prentice Hall, Inc., 1966.

Puner, Helen Walker. *Freud: His Life and His Mind*. New York: Howell Soskin, 1947.

Rickman, John (ed.). Sigmund Freud (Civilization, War and Death). London: The Hogarth Press, 1968.

Rieff, Philip. Freud, The Mind of the Moralist. New York: The Viking Press, 1959.

Roazen, Paul. Freud, Political and Social Thought. New York: Alfred A. Knopf, 1968.

Rosen, George. "Freud and Medicine in Vienna." Miller, Jonathan, ed. Freud: The Man, His World, His Influence. Boston: Little, Brown and Co., 1972.

Sahakian, William S. and Sahakian, Mabel Lewis. Plato. Boston: G. K. Hall and Co., 1977.

Schacht, Richard. Alienation. Garden City, New York: Doubleday, 1971.

Schneider, Louis. The Freudian Psychology and Veblen's Social Theory. New York: King's Crown Press, 1948, p. 54.

Schoenwald, Richard. Freud, The Man and His Mind. New York: Alfred A. Knopf, 1956.

Shaw, Clifford. The Jack Roller. Chicago: University of Chicago Press, 1930.

Strupp, Hans H. Freud and Modern Psychoanalysis. Woodbury, New York: Barron's Educational Series, Inc., 1967.

Szasz, Thomas S. "Freud as a Leader" in Cioffi, Frank, ed. Freud: Modern Judgments. London: Macmillan, 1973.

Szasz, Thomas S. The Myth Of Mental Illness. New York: Hoeber-Harper, 1961.

Thomas, W. I. and Znaniecki, F. The Polish Peasant in Europe and America. 2nd ed. New York: A. A. Knopf, 1927.

Trilling, Lionel. Freud and the Crisis of our Culture. Boston: The Beacon Press, 1955.

Turner, Ralph. "Collective Behavior" Faris, Robert E., ed. Handbook of Modern Sociology, Chicago: Rand-McNally, 1964.

Weber, Max. The Protestant Ethic and the Spirit of Capitalism. trans. by Talcott Parsons, New York: Scribners, 1930.

Whyte, Lancelot L. The Unconscious Before Freud. Garden City: New York: Doubleday Anchor Books, 1962.

Wittles, Fritz. Freud and His Time. New York: Liveright, 1931.

Wortis, Joseph. Fragment of an Analysis with Freud. New York: Simon and Schuster, 1954.

Zilboorg, Gregory. A History of Medical Psychology. New York: Norton, 1941.

Journals

Axelrad, Sidney. "Juvenile Delinquency: A Study of the Relationship between Psychoanalysis and Sociology," Smith College Studies in Social Work, February 1965, 35, 2, pp. 89-109.

Bergen, Bernard J. and Rosenberg, Stanley I. "The New Neo-Freudians: Psychoanalytic Dimensions of Social Change," Psychiatry, No. 1, February 1971, Vol. 34, pp. 19-37.

Bernfeld, S. "Freud's Earliest Theories and the School of Helmholtz," Psychoanalytic Quarterly, XIII, July 1944, pp. 341-362.

Bocock, R. J. "Freud and the Centrality of Instincts in Psychoanalytic Sociology," British Journal of Sociology, December 1977, 28, 4, pp. 467-480.

Burgess, E. W. "The Influence of Sigmund Freud Upon Sociology in the United States," American Journal of Sociology 45, November 1939, pp. 356-374.

Eliot, Thomas I. "A Psychoanalytic Interpretation of Group Formation and Behavior," American Journal Of Sociology 26, November 1920, pp. 333-352.

Faris, E. "Are Instincts Data or Hypotheses?" American Journal of Sociology, XXVIII, September 1921, pp. 184-196.

Faris, E. "Ethnological Light on Psychological Problems." Publications of the American Sociological Society, XVI, 1922, pp. 113-120.

Fulkerson, Stephen V. "Psychoanalytic Influences on Social Science," Social Science, 38, 2, April 1963, pp. 83-91.

Halla, Frank L. "Childhood, Culture & Society in Psychoanalysis and History," The Historian, Vol. XXXIX, No. 3, May 1977, pp. 423-438.

Holmes, Roger. "Freud and Social Class," British Journal of Sociology, 16, 1, March 1965, pp. 48-67.

Jones, Ernest. "Sigmund Freud," International Journal of Psychoanalysis, 21, 1940, pp. 1-26.

Jones, Robert A. "Freud and American Sociology, 1909-1949," Journal of the History of the Behavioral Sciences, 10, 1, January 1974, pp. 21-39.

Mora, G. "The Historiography of Psychiatry and Its Development: A Re-evaluation," Journal of the History of the Behavioral Sciences, Vol. 1, 1965, pp. 43-52.

Ogburn, W. F. "Bias, Psychoanalysis and the Subjective in Relation to the Social Sciences," Publications of the American Sociological Society, XVII, 1923, pp. 62-74.

Parsons, Talcott. "Social Structure and the Development of Personality: Freud's Contribution to the Integration of Psychology and Sociology," Psychiatry, XXI, No. 4, November 1958, pp. 321-340.

Wrong, Dennis. "The Over-socialized Conception of Man in Modern Sociology." American Sociological Review, Vol. 26, April 1961, pp. 183-193.

INDEX

Aggression, 31, 58, 59, 64, 65, 72, 75, 76, 77-80, 82, 85-87, 89, 90-91, 94, 97, 109, 114, 128, 138, 141, 160, 164, 166, 168, 169, 174, 175, 177
  organically based, 87,
  redirected, 178
Aim-inhibited relationships, 75, 78, 105, 110, 114
Alexander, Franz, 23, 44
Allegorical and analogical reasoning, 68, 80, 81, 89, 91, 92, 94, 96, 106-107, 110
Ambivalence, 28, 57, 59, 65, 96, 112, 114, 118, 119, 129, 130, 131, 134, 164
  child's toward parent, 96, 118-119, 127, 132, 156, 164
  Freud's toward own father, 28
  toward Judaism, 28
  and mother love, 77
Animism (see Religion)
Anti-semitism, 25, 27, 33, 37, 40, 86, 115, 139, 161
Anxiety, as defense, 55, 128
Arlow, Jacob, 40, 47, 111, 143
Art as socially cohesive, 77
Atheism, 17, 20, 136-138
Authority, 113, 114, 117, 119, 120, 124, 137, 141, 173, 174
  critique of Freud's view, 174
  related to guilt, 132
  individual's need of, 176
  internalized, 173, 177
  prior to love, 173
  prior to morality, 173

Authority (continued)
  patriarchal, 164-165, 173, 174, 177
  religious, 139, 140
  social function of, 174
  socialization to, 138, 159, 173, 178
  ubiquitous, 177
Autobiographical Study, An, 19, 21, 25, 26-27, 31, 35, 36, 43, 44, 45, 46, 51, 69, 100

Bagehot, Walter, 85
Bakan, David, 149, 180
Benedict, Ruth, 125, 145
Bentham, Jeremy, 53, 160
Bernard, L.L., 10
Bernfeld, S., 50, 61
Bierstedt, Robert, 167, 173, 181
Biological man, 158-159, 178
Bourgeoisie, 14, 16, 86, 173
Breuer, Joseph, 31, 36, 51
Brickner, Richard M., 103
Brown, J. A. C., 65-66
Brücke, Ernst, 28, 29, 50
Bruner, Jerome, 41, 47, 152, 180
Buddhist ideal, 94
Bureaucracy, 113, 159
Burgess, Ernest W., 4, 10
Burke, Kenneth, 126, 145

Capitalism, 94, 124, 126, 157, 160, 164, 166, 170, 171, 173
Carus, Carl G., 24
Cassirer, Ernst, 50, 61
Catharsis, 31
Charcot, Jean, 30
Causality, principle of, 160-161
Chodorow, Nancy, 124-125, 145

Civilization and its Discontents, 59, 64, 70, 71, 72, 73-74, 76, 77, 78, 79, 80, 81, 83, 85, 86, 87, 89-90, 100, 101, 102, 103, 114, 121, 122, 123, 137, 144, 145, 146, 153, 154, 180
Clan, 57, 65
Class consciousness, 17, 160, 165, 168, 169, 170, 171
Cognitive processes, 72, 76, 89, 90, 111, 151, 152, 178
Collective consciousness, 66
  mind, 68, 106-107
  representations, 107, 141, 176
Collins, Randall, 6, 7, 11, 24-25, 44
Communion (holy) and totem feast, 132
Comte, August, 16, 85, 91, 137, 138, 142, 167, 168
Condorcet, Marquis de, 16, 50
Conflict, internal, 13, 22, 24, 31, 51, 54, 55, 56, 74, 89, 92, 94, 96, 159, 167, 168, 170
  sexual, 31, 121, 122
  social, 17, 18, 51, 59, 64, 66, 72-74, 76, 83, 89, 94, 95-96, 97, 98, 121, 161, 166, 168, 169, 170, 173
  unconscious, 31, 51, 54
  within the psychoanalytic movement, 37, 38, 39
Conscience (see also Superego), 19, 114, 123, 125, 159
  origin of, 119, 130, 138
Cooley, Charles H., 4, 67, 70, 167
Cultural adaptability, 118
Cultural Superego (see Superego)
Cuzzort, R. P., 6, 11

Darwin, Charles, x, 1, 17, 27, 35, 64, 127, 152, 167, 173
Darwinism, 13, 17, 18, 19, 23, 92-94, 152, 165, 167, 168, 173
  Social Darwinism, 18, 85, 92, 94, 173
Death instinct, 79, 166
Decker, Hannah, 22, 24, 40, 44, 47
Definition of the situation, 139
Delusion distinguished from illusion, 134-135
Determinism, 41, 50, 52, 57, 89, 97, 125, 160-161, 165, 168
  biological, 158
de Tocquiville, Alexis, 85
Diderot, Denis, 13
Displacement, 20, 152
"Dora," case of, 157
Drives, 55, 56, 59, 65, 72, 75, 78, 89, 151, 166, 169, 170, 171, 177
  aim-inhibited, 75, 78, 79, 105, 109
  characteristics of, 54-55
  erotic, 123, 170, 177
  pleasure-oriented, 133
Durkheim, Emile, x, 66, 72, 75, 107, 131, 138, 139, 140-142, 150, 176

Economic man, 157, 175
Ego, 20, 24, 53, 54, 55, 58, 79, 80, 106, 111, 114, 118, 126, 156, 162, 164
  conflict with id, 167
  defenses, 55, 56, 110
  differentiated from id, 156, 161, 165
  ideal, 105-106, 111, 112, 114
Einstein, Albert, ix, 33, 75, 84, 86, 98, 166
Eliot, Thomas D., 10

Ellenberger, Henri, 13, 15, 16, 18, 19, 20, 24, 30, 36, 37, 38, 40, 43, 44, 45, 46, 47, 131, 146
Empiricism, 2, 4, 33, 138, 150, 160, 174
Enlightenment, 13, 14-15, 16, 17, 40, 50, 165, 167, 168
and its Weltanschauung, 15
Erikson, Erik, 70, 120, 144
Eros, 16, 52, 67, 76, 79, 94, 121
in conflict with Thanatos, 79, 94
Esslin, Martin, 29, 33, 45
European intellectual history, 13-20
Exogamy, 58, 64, 65, 131

Family, 95, 105, 116-127, 154, 175
decline of authority, 174
and father, 112, 164, 168, 176
critique of Freud's views, 122-127, 164-165
Freud's theory of origins, 121, 123, 168, 169
functions, 123, 177
nuclear, 124, 176
of orientation, 160
paradigm of society, 116-117, 138, 164, 173, 174, 176
power relationships within, 120, 164
prototype of authority and power, 120, 164, 174, 177
socializing agent, 116-117, 120, 174, 177
and state, 194
structure, 115, 116, 123, 124, 164, 177
threats to civilization, 121, 164
western patriarchal, 126, 153, 164-165, 176, 177
and women's role, 122, 168

Faris, Ellsworth, 4, 10
Father, (see also Leader), 58, 64, 65, 67, 69, 88, 97, 106, 112, 113, 115, 117, 119, 121, 123, 124, 128-129, 130, 132, 135, 141, 171, 176
ambivalence toward, 65, 81, 96, 112-113, 115, 131, 132
Jesus Christ as representative, 81, 132
primal, 106, 112, 119, 131, 132, 134, 141
as religious object, 138
as socializing agent, 117, 119, 164
as totem equivalent, 131
Ferenczi, Sandor, 39
Fliess, Wilhelm. 41
Frazer, Sir James, 69, 91, 131
Free association, 31
Freud, Ernst, 30, 45
Freud, Sigmund,
ahistorical viewpoint, 124, 176
use of allegory and analogy, 68, 80, 81, 89, 91, 92, 94, 96, 106-107, 110, 152, 153, 173, 176
as collector, 32
as linguist, 8, 28, 55
as stage theorist, 70, 155
attitude toward Jewishness, 28, 37, 41
attitude toward medicine, 21, 34-35
attitude toward religion, 17, 129, 136-137, 139 170
attitude toward science, 17
attitude toward Soviet state, 17, 74, 86, 89
attitude toward U.S., ix, 32, 37, 85
attitude toward women ix, 35, 37, 38, 40, 122, 157, 171

Freud (continued)
  awareness of culture, 7, 35, 69, 88, 139, 156, 157, 175
  belief in the patriarchy 37, 38, 40, 115, 124, 176
  break with Breuer, 31, 51
  clinical contributions to social science, 56-57
  cocaine discovery, 30
  compared with Beethoven, x
  compared with Copernicus, 1
  compared with Darwin, 1
  compared with Erikson and Piaget, 70
  contrasted to Cooley, 4, 67, 70
  contrasted to Durkheim, 66, 72, 75, 107, 139-142, 165-172, 176
  contrasted to Hobbes, 66, 166, 173-174
  contrasted to Marxist view of society, 67, 74, 89, 96, 97, 139-142, 165-172, 176
  considered by Parsons, 5, 161-163
  desire for fame, 26, 30, 30, 35, 38, 41, 161, 179
  determinism, 89, 160-161
  early career, 29-31, 154
  early years, 25-27, 40
  education, 26
  effects of anti-Semitism, 26, 27, 37, 40, 139, 161
  effects of Nazism, 26
  ethnocentrism, 166, 176
  final illness, x, 34
  Hannibal fantasies, 26, 27
  influence of Darwinism, 17, 18, 19, 27, 35, 64, 92-94, 127, 165-167, 168
  influence of Enlightenment, 15, 40, 165
  influence of Goethe, 27

Freud (continued)
  influence of Nietzsche, 19, 81
  influence of Vienna, 28-29, 33, 40, 139
  in the U.S., 32
  later fame, ix, 33, 36
  male domination, 18-19, 37, 40, 115, 124, 171
  marginal status, 27, 36, 40, 41, 139, 161
  medical education, 27, 28
  need for fealty, 38, 40
  personal characteristics, 34-41, 94, 122, 161, 176
  privileged position in family, 26, 40
  problems of translation, 8
  psychological reductionism, 150
  relationship to wife (Martha Bernays), 29-30, 37
  sampling error, 176
  self-identification with Moses, 28, 37, 38, 97
  sense of isolation, 32, 35-36
  theory of the self, 53, 54, 175
Fromm, Erich, 27, 28, 38, 39, 45, 46
Functionalism, 5, 125, 134, 142, 152, 163
Future of an Illusion, The, 58-59, 70, 77, 78, 82, 83, 84-85, 94, 98, 100, 101, 102, 103, 104, 127, 129-130, 133, 134-135, 136, 137, 145, 146, 156, 161, 181

Galdston, Iago, 21, 41, 44, 47, 51, 61, 150, 180
Generalized other, 6, 53
  and superego, 6
Gerth, Hans, 6, 11
Glover, Jonathan, 125, 145
God(s), 59, 92, 129, 134

God(s) (continued)
 as father, 58, 128-130, 132, 133, 134, 138, 141
 a hoax, 138
 origin of, 131, 136, 141
Goethe, Johann V., 27, 36
 prize, 33, 152
Goffman, Erving, 120, 144, 151, 154, 160, 180
Gouldner, Alvin, 5, 11, 163, 181
Great man theory (see also Leader), 64, 75
Greek, drama, x
 ideal, 94
Group,
 as extension of family, 115
 critique of Freuds's theory of, 115-116
 defined by Freud, 114, 116
 mind, 105, 108, 109, 111, 114
 primary, 4, 106
 psychology, defined by Freud, 106
 ties, 58, 75, 105-106, 110, 115
Group Psychology and the Analysis of the Ego, 58, 67, 100, 105, 106, 107, 110, 111, 112, 114, 116, 127, 139, 143, 144, 145, 152, 153, 156, 173, 180, 181, 182
Guilt, 58, 59, 63, 64-65, 66, 67, 68-69, 75, 80, 92, 119, 126, 128, 130-131, 134, 135-136, 141, 159, 171, 175
 related to authority, 132
 inherited, 155, 176
 related to morality, 132, 170
 primeval, 176
 as socializing force, 119, 125-126, 159

Hallowell, A. I. 20-21
Hartmann, Eduard von, 24-25

Hefner, Richard, 85, 102
Hegel, Georg, 124, 168
Helmholtz, Hermann, 50, 150
Hinkle, Gisela, 2, 4, 10
Hobbes, Nicholas, 18, 66, 68, 74, 78, 125, 133, 166, 173-174
Hobbesian question, 176
Holistic approach to man, 150-151
Hypnosis, 30, 31, 58
Hysteria 30
 and sexual conflict, 31

Id 20, 24, 53, 54, 94, 156, 161
 in conflict with ego, 167
 in conflict with superego, 94, 170
 replaced by ego, 161, 165
Ideal type, 159
Identification, 7, 58, 75, 76, 77, 78, 84, 85, 105-106, 114-115, 119, 123, 125, 126, 151, 159, 177
 antecedent to love, 173
 as form of love, 173
 role in socialization, 151, 177, 178
 in superego formation, 119, 123, 125, 156, 120, 177
Illusion, distinguished from delusion, 134-135
Immortality, 130
Impression management, 120
Incest taboo, 65, 73, 131, 134, 164
Individual development, 93, 108-109, 110, 112-113, 114, 117-118, 135, 138, 154, 164, 173
 and need of love, 176
Individual extrapolated to society, 71, 74, 75-76, 89, 92, 93, 97, 105, 107, 112, 115, 135, 138, 173, 175

Individual-society analogy,
    63, 67, 70, 74, 80, 81,
    87, 88, 89, 91, 92, 106,
    107, 117, 173
Industrial revolution, 16, 17
Infantile sexuality, 32, 117-
    118, 174,
  as social role, 162
Inheritance of traits (see
    also Lamarckism), 67-68,
    75, 105, 107-109, 118,
    128, 141, 154, 176
Instinct, 4, 8, 16, 19, 25,
    54, 55, 58, 65, 69, 72,
    73, 76, 78, 79, 80, 82,
    83, 84, 85, 86, 90, 109,
    112, 117, 118, 119, 122,
    128, 133, 135, 156, 159,
    170
Interpretation of Dreams, The,
    6, 25, 32
Introductory Lectures in
    Psychoanalysis, 95, 103
Izenberg, Gerald, 21, 44, 49,
    50, 61, 164-165, 181

James, William, 138
Jesus Christ, 81, 132
  related to Moses and primal
    father, 132
Jones, Ernest, 15, 16, 23, 32,
    35, 37, 38, 43, 44, 45,
    46, 157, 181
Jung, Carl, 38, 39

Kant, Immanuel, 22
Kaufmann, Walter, 19, 20
King, E. W., 6, 11
Kuhn, Thomas, 1, 10

Labeling perspective, 89, 90
Lamarckism, 69, 108, 115,
    155, 176
Latency, 6, 120
Lauzen, Gerald, 26, 32, 33,
    34, 45, 46, 57, 61

Leader, 58, 75, 81, 83-85,
    94, 95, 97, 105-106,
    110, 111, 112, 113, 115-
    116, 117, 120, 173
  ambivalence toward, 65, 96,
    112, 115
  charismatic, 83
  as ego ideal, 105, 106, 111
  as father person, 58, 59-
    60, 64, 94, 112, 115
  as love object, 173
Le Bon, Gustave, 58, 111
Le Mettrie, D., 50
Levitt, Morton, 20, 35, 43,
    46
Libido, 52, 64, 73, 74, 75,
    76, 79, 91, 94, 105-106,
    109, 110, 113, 114, 115,
    120, 128, 176, 177
  and cultural demands, 121
  and differences between men
    and women, 122
  exchange, 178
  infantile 174
Locke, John 166
Love, 73-76, 78, 80, 87, 109-
    110, 114, 117, 118, 119,
    121, 125, 166, 168, 173,
    176
  opposed to narcissism, 110
  romantic, 126
  self-love (narcissism), 110,
    114, 115
  as socializing agent, 117-
    119, 123, 162, 174, 178,
  and women, 122, 168

Machiavelli, Niccolo, 114
MacIntyre, Alasdair, 67, 100
Makowski, M., 11, 24-25, 44,
    67
Male role definition, 125
Malinowski, Bronislaw, 4, 11,
    34
Malthus, Thomas, 18
Mann, Thomas, 12, 33
Mannheim, Karl, 138

Martindale, Don, 5, 6, 11, 152, 180
Marx, Karl, x, 17, 89, 96, 129, 160, 165-167, 168-172, 174
Marxism, 13, 17, 74, 89, 94, 96, 97, 160, 165-167
  compared with Freudian thought, 165-167, 168-172
Materialism, 20, 28, 41, 50, 165, 171
Mead, George H., 6, 53, 72, 89, 162
  and the self, 53, 167
Mead, Margaret, 4, 11
Mental illness, 20
  organic in nature, 14, 22, 23
  psychodynamic causality, 51
  as psychological phenomenon, 22
  as disturbance of reason, 14
  punishment for sin, 22
  as social phenomenon, 6, 7
  related to the unconscious, 19
Mental symptoms, as expression of conflict, 31
Merton, Robert, 6, 11, 152, 180
Mill, John Stuart, 16, 37
Mills, C. Wright, 6, 11
Mind, collective, 106-107
  evolution of, 92
  conceived by G. H. Mead, 53
  conceived by Nietzsche, 20
  as organic structure, 20
  primitive, 154
  as social product, 53
  structural theory of, 53
Mind-altering substances, 77
Mind-body dualism, 130
Mora, G. 23
Moral autonomy, 126
Morality, 58, 63, 65, 125, 126, 129, 130, 176

Morality (continued)
  Freud's theory of origins, 126, 131
  as expression of guilt, 65, 68, 125-126, 132
  pragmatic basis, 133
  and religion, 128, 131, 132, 133, 137, 142
Morris, Desmond, 155, 181
Moses and Monotheism, 4, 28, 32, 34, 46, 59-60, 64, 65, 91, 97, 100, 103, 105, 107, 108, 112-113, 117, 127, 131-132, 134, 143, 144, 146, 153, 180
Moses, related to Jesus, 132
Mother, as social object, 162

Nazism, 33, 38
Neurath, Otto, 126
Neurosis,
  as asocial behavior, 87-88
  as cultural malady, 89-90
  growing prevalence, 137, 170
  historical changes in form, 139-140
  individual, 77, 87, 92, 97 137
  obsessional, 134, 135, 136
  parallel to primitive taboos, 134
  purposive nature of, 50, 87
  replaced by unhappiness, 172
  as self-alienation, 88
  sexual theory of, 32, 51
  as social act, 88, 97
Newton, Sir Isaac, 14
Nietzsche, Friedrich, 13, 19, 20, 43, 81
  thought, 14, 19, 20, 81
Norms, 54, 56, 68, 95, 98, 112, 114, 118, 119, 126, 133, 137, 159, 163, 164, 176, 177

Norms (continued)
  derived from social conditions, 7, 169
  emergent, 112
  group, 114
  ideal, 159-160
  internalization, 118, 120, 163
  invested with sacred meaning, 141, 142
  peer group, 174
  related to guilt, 119

Object relations 54, 70, 73, 106, 128, 161, 162, 163, 173, 177
Oedipus complex, 7, 18, 28, 32, 96, 111, 112, 114, 115, 116, 118-119, 124, 125, 134, 135, 141, 154, 156, 173
  as power struggle, 120
  related to totemism, 131, 134
  resolution of, 163
  sociological implications, 163
Ogburn, William F., 3, 10
On the History of the Psychoanalytic Movement, 39
Organic solidarity, 72
Original sin, 131, 141, 160, 171

Pareto, Vilfredo, 5
Park, Robert E., 4, 10
Parricide (patricide), 58, 63, 64, 65, 66, 67, 68, 69, 75, 112, 128, 131, 132, 141, 155, 160, 169, 171, 174
Parsons, Talcott, 5, 11, 151-152, 161-163, 180, 181
  critique of Freud, 161-163
Participant observation, 153, 154

Pasteur, Louis, 21, 49
Personality, 52
  as behavioral dynamism, 52
Philosophy, 21
  and psychopathology, 22
Piaget, Jean, 70
Plato, 39, 76, 84, 109, 165, 174
Pleasure principle, 67, 71, 72, 73, 98, 117, 128, 133, 162, 166
Polarities, 87, 88, 121, 160, 167
  law of, 15-16
  and Romanticism, 15
Positivism, 5, 13, 16, 17, 19, 28, 52, 137, 149-150, 167
Primal Father (see Father)
Primal horde, 18, 57, 58, 63, 64, 67, 68, 69, 106, 110, 112, 126-127, 131, 132, 174
  as heuristic device, 126-127
  history of Freud's use, 152-153
Primary group, 4, 106
Progress, idea of, 3, 14, 17, 19, 91, 92-94, 96, 97-98, 137, 154, 167, 171-172
Proletariat, 16, 17
Psychiatry, 14, 90
  definition of mental illness, 90
  dynamic 31
  product of the Enlightenment, 14
  Romantic to Scientific, 21-24
Psychic, apparatus, 52
  conflict, 56, 136
  continuity (see also Inheritance of traits), 68, 107-108, 154-155
  determinism, 3, 52, 57, 160-161
  energy, 52, 55

Psychic (continued)
  equilibrium, 55
  processes within groups, 105-116
  residues, 155
Psychoanalysis, 32, 99
  assumptions, 161
  and causality, 160-161
  current status, 149
  and free association, 31
  as a movement, 34, 36, 38-39
  as an outgrowth of organic medicine, 49-50
  as a paradox, 178-179
  as form of religion, 38-39, 140
  resistance from social scientists, 149-150
  and Romantic medicine, 36, 150
  and sociology, 2-7, 151, 155-156, 161-163
  success in the U.S., 32-33
Psychological reductionism, 150-155

Reality, as derivative, 155
  orientation, 93, 129, 136, 174
  principle, 67, 70, 71, 72, 98, 117, 128, 136, 162
  public and private, 151
  social construction of, 53, 54, 56, 59, 70, 71, 88, 90, 163
  socially preexisting, 151, 156, 162, 168, 177
  testing, 106, 111
Recapitulation, biological doctrine of, 154
Reductionism, psychological, 150, 158
  sociological, 158
Reification, 153

Religion, 14, 17, 20, 40, 58, 59, 65, 77, 91-92, 93, 113, 127-142, 152, 161, 171, 175, 176
  critical of status quo, 139
  decline of belief, 136-137
  descended from totemism, 131-132
  Durkheim's views, 131, 138-142
  faith contrasted with structure, 139
  father deity to son, 132
  genesis of, 138, 169
  and guilt, 132, 136
  as ideology, 170
  as illusion, 128, 134, 136, 138, 165, 170
  and morality, 128, 133, 170
  a universal neurosis, 128, 134, 135, 136
  protection against antisocial drives, 135, 136, 170
  against individual neurosis, 135
  psychoanalysis as form of, 140
  and rites of passage, 142
  social utility of, 138-142
  versus science, 20, 58, 137, 165
  and the transcendental, 142
  as will of the father, 133, 138, 170
  as wish-fulfillment, 135, 138
Repression, 4, 32, 33, 51, 54, 55, 66, 70, 72, 76, 77, 92, 98, 111, 112, 133, 135
  organically determined, 69
  related to socialization, 92, 116, 125, 176, 177

Repression (continued)
  as societal force, 165, 166, 173
  versus sexuality, 69
Rieff, Phillip, ix, 53, 54, 61, 95, 97, 103, 104, 138, 139-140, 146
Roazen, Paul, x, 114, 144

Saint Paul, 109
St. Simon, Claude de, 16
Schneider, Louis, 5, 11
Schopenhauer, Arthur, 24
Science, 77, 91-92, 93, 128, 136, 137, 138, 142, 149, 160, 167, 178
  and causality, 160
  opposed to religion, 20
Scientism, 17, 19, 20, 40, 41, 139, 168, 171-172
Self, arising from id-ego conflict, 167
  and society, 53, 54, 71-72 167, 173
  theory of, 53, 54, 167, 173, 177
Sexual division of labor, 124-125
Sexual drive, 52, 56, 58, 65, 69, 75, 76, 86, 91, 106, 109, 168, 173
  and aggression, 77-78, 169
  and family legitimation, 121, 123, 168
Sexual drive (continued)
  in man, 121, 169
  opposed by economic factors, 121-122
  opposed to social solidarity, 111, 121, 164, 169
  redirected, 178
Shaw, Clifford, 10
Simmel, Georg, 41-42
Smith, Adam, 94
Social change, 90-99, 137, 139, 161, 171, 174

Social cohesion, 63-65, 66, 67, 69, 70, 72, 73, 75, 76-77, 84, 85-86, 98, 107, 113-114, 115, 116, 133, 141, 159
  based on emotional factors, 173-174
  and freedom, 174
  through identification, 173, 177
Social contract, 14, 15, 63, 65, 66, 68-69, 74, 78, 86-87, 166-167, 168, 174
Social control, 63-66, 72, 73, 75, 76, 82-83, 95, 99, 113, 116, 119-120, 133, 137, 139, 141, 142, 159, 169, 173, 174, 178
  and charismatic father, 176
Social evolution (see also Progress, idea of), 19, 91, 92, 95, 96, 137, 139, 154, 155, 161, 167, 168, 171
Social groups, 105-116, 176
Social institutions, as adaptive processes, 87, 133, 169, 177
  as cognitive responses, 89
Social origins, 18, 57, 63-65, 67, 68, 155, 169, 175
Socialization, 6, 81, 92, 116-119, 174
  as affective process, 177, 178
  and erotic drives, 123, 162, 177
  and identification, 151, 151, 163, 177, 178
  over--, 159
  parental roles, 117-119, 162-163, 177
  related to power and authority, 117-120, 138, 159
  related to repression, 92, 116, 170, 176
  under--, 119-120, 159, 178

Social stratification, 63, 75, 84, 94, 95, 105, 112-113, 115, 124, 137, 165, 166, 169, 170-172, 176
Social systems perspective in social science, ix
Sociological, interest in psychoanalysis, 1-7
and the irrational, 178
perspective, 67, 88, 151 157
contrasted with psychological, 70-71, 75, 88, 151, 155-156, 161-163
in need of refinement, 178
resistance to psychoanalysis, 4, 149-150, 178
Spencer, Herbert, 16, 91
Spengler, Oswald, 81
Stress-adaptation syndrome, 52
Studies in Hysteria, 31
Superego, 6, 53, 54, 55, 58, 70, 80-82, 89, 94, 111, 114, 115, 117, 119, 141, 152, 156, 159, 161, 164, 177, 178
conflict with id, 94, 117, 170
cultural superego, 80-82, 97, 119, 161
deficiencies, 178
group, 115
and Mead's generalized other, 6
Symbolic interactionism, 72
Sublimation, 3, 55-56, 58, 64, 83, 94, 151, 166, 168, 171, 173, 178
Szasz, Thomas, 42, 47, 90, 103

Thanatos, 16, 94
conflict with Eros, 94

Thermodynamics, first law of, 52
Three Essays on the Theory of Sexuality, 69, 100
Thomas, William I., 3-4, 10, 36
Totem and Taboo, 28, 32, 57-58, 59, 64, 66, 67, 68, 69, 70, 73, 85, 91, 92, 96, 100, 101, 103, 105, 106-107, 111, 127, 129, 131, 132, 142, 143, 145, 146, 150, 152, 174, 182
Totemism, 58, 65, 128, 131, 141
father equivalent, 131
forerunner of religion, 131-132
Transference, 88
Trieb, 8, 55
Trilling, Lionel, 158, 181
Trotter, Wilfred, 110
Turner, Ralph, 112, 144

Unconscious, 3, 13, 17, 19, 20, 24-25, 31, 32, 35, 53, 57, 88, 107, 169, 175
conflict, 31, 51
motivation, 51, 169
processes, 52, 56, 107
Undersocialization, 119-120
Utilitarianism 53, 73, 86, 120, 160, 167
opposed to libido, 120

Values construction, 126, 138, 151, 157, 163
derivative of social conditions, 169
prior to needs, 157
produced by unconscious forces, 169
as social goals, 112
sources of, 157
Veblen, Thorstein, 175
and economic man, 175

Vitalism, 22, 23, 51

War, 75, 76, 86, 95-96, 99, 101, 125, 166
  root cause, 86
  solution to, 99
Weber, Max, 75, 94, 103, 113, 116, 159
Wells, Herbert, G., 34
Weltanschauung, 8, 107, 160
  of Enlightenment and Romanticism, 15
  scientific, 142
Whyte, Lancelot L., 25, 44
Wittels, Fritz, 36, 46

Women, change in sex roles, 125
  defined sex roles, 124-125, 171
  influence of environment, 157
  relation to civilization, 122
  subordinate position, 18, 37
Work, 18, 35, 58, 72-73, 77, 78, 79, 82, 94-95, 109, 121, 122, 151, 157, 170
Wortis, Joseph, 37, 46
Wrong, Dennis, 158-159, 181
Wundt, Wilhelm, 131

Zilboorg, Gregory, 23, 44
Znaniecki, Florian, 3-4, 10

ABOUT THE AUTHOR

Arthur K. Berliner, a graduate of the City College of New York, has a Master's degree in Social Work from Case Western Reserve University and a Ph.D. in Sociology from North Texas State University. He has worked with substance abusers, the mentally ill, and federal offenders in clinical and correctional settings.

Dr. Berliner has published about twenty-five papers in professional journals, dealing with treatment of alcohol and narcotic abuse, mental health, corrections, and human services coordination and administration. He has co-authored a monograph on integrating institution and community treatment and follow-up of narcotic addicts, and edited a book, The Family in Texas. Since 1975 he has been Director of the Social Work Program of Texas Christian University where he is an Associate Professor in the Department of Sociology.

108993

DATE DUE

NOV 28 '88			
DEC 4 '89			
DE 19 '94			
SE 25 '97			
DE 12			
AP 27 99			
DE 06 02			

```
BF                  108993
173
.F85     Berliner, Arthur K.
B43          Psychoanalysis and society :
1983
```

HIEBERT LIBRARY
Fresno Pacific College - M. B. Seminary
Fresno, Calif. 93702

DEMCO